COMING
through the
VALLEY

COMING
through the
VALLEY

DAVID RAYNOR

XULON PRESS

Xulon Press
2301 Lucien Way #415
Maitland, FL 32751
407.339.4217
www.xulonpress.com

© 2022 by David Raynor

All rights reserved solely by the author. The author guarantees all contents are original and do not infringe upon the legal rights of any other person or work. No part of this book may be reproduced in any form without the permission of the author.

Due to the changing nature of the Internet, if there are any web addresses, links, or URLs included in this manuscript, these may have been altered and may no longer be accessible. The views and opinions shared in this book belong solely to the author and do not necessarily reflect those of the publisher. The publisher therefore disclaims responsibility for the views or opinions expressed within the work.

Unless otherwise indicated, Scripture quotations taken from the Holy Bible, New International Version (NIV). Copyright © 1973, 1978, 1984, 2011 by Biblica, Inc.™. Used by permission. All rights reserved.

Scripture quotations taken from the Holy Bible, New Living Translation (NLT). Copyright ©1996, 2004, 2007 by Tyndale House Foundation. Used by permission of Tyndale House Publishers, Inc.

Scripture quotations taken from The Message (MSG). Copyright © 1993, 1994, 1995, 1996, 2000, 2001, 2002. Used by permission of NavPress Publishing Group. Used by permission. All rights reserved.

Paperback ISBN-13: 978-1-66286-574-9
Ebook ISBN-13: 978-1-66286-575-6

ACKNOWLEDGEMENTS

MY ORIGINAL PURPOSE in writing this was as a kind of personal therapy, although I had thought my family might benefit from reading it. On a sudden whim – or more likely a prompting from God – I asked a wise friend to look at the manuscript and give me his opinion.

Dr Roger Aubrey is a widely-respected Bible teacher and author. I knew he would be totally honest: there would be no flannel or flattery. What I did not expect was the amount of editing and the number of suggestions that he offered. And yes, he was quite sure that the thing should be published. Without Roger's input, I might still be in a kind of hesitant limbo; so I gratefully acknowledge his part in turning this into a short book.

I also put on record my great gratitude to the dozens of medical practitioners and others who unfailingly did their best for Gwen in her incurable condition: general practitioners, hospital doctors, consultants, specialist nurses, palliative nurses, district nurses, therapists of various kinds, dieticians, paramedics and carers. The staff at Queenscourt Hospice in Southport U.K. – always Gwen's first choice 'departure lounge' – combined meticulous care with perfect timing, even in the midst of the Covid pandemic with its tiresome lockdowns. She was admitted in late November 2020 for two weeks of 'observation and respite care', and she passed away on the final afternoon of those two weeks.

To my family, Gwen's family and the many Christians who prayed for us throughout her illness and beyond – especially my dear friends in the Community Church in Southport – you know who you are and I am so blessed by you all: thank you!

Table of Contents

Acknowledgements v
1. When the landscape changed.................... 1
2. Sympathy or compassion? 9
3. Breaking it to the boys....................... 13
4. To the wider family 17
5. Over to the experts 21
6. The God who heals 25
7. John Wimber at Wembley 33
8. Help from the medics 37
9. An enjoyable interlude 43
10. Help from the hospice........................ 47
11. Hospital procedures......................... 53
12. Appointments............................... 57
13. Therapies....................................61
14. The feeding tube............................ 65
15. District nurses 69

16. No Covid, just MND 73
17. Carers in the house 79
18. Steady deterioration 83
19. Into the hospice 89
20. The agony ends................................ 95
21. Good things to remember 101
22. A simple cremation 107
23. Celebration at last 111
24. Grief and gratitude 115
25. Making adjustments 119
26. One year on 125
27. Looking forward 129
28. How to mourn? 133
29. Exploring emotions........................... 137
30. What of the future? 145
31. Final reflections 149

1. When the landscape changed

'We can rejoice, too, when we run into problems and trials, for we know that they are good for us – they help us learn to endure. And endurance develops strength of character in us, and character strengthens our confident expectation of salvation. And this expectation will not disappoint us. For we know how dearly God loves us, because he has given us the Holy Spirit to fill our hearts with his love.'
[Romans 5: 3-5 New Living Translation]

WE HAD EAGERLY anticipated the day. Saturday 21st July 2018 was the start of our annual Bible Week, a gathering of over a thousand Christians at the Nottinghamshire Showground just outside Newark. Bible Weeks were special: times of spiritual refreshing and energising; time at leisure with like-minded people; time given to worshipping God in dimensions not often seen on other occasions; time to be taught and challenged by apostles, prophets and teachers of the Word of God.

On the way to Newark, we were calling in at Aintree Hospital in Liverpool to have the results of Gwen's neurological tests. The random twitching of muscles in various parts of her arms and legs had given cause for concern. The fingers of her left hand were permanently bent towards the palm and she had lost much of the gripping power in that hand.

The doctor was unemotional as he said, 'It's not good news, I'm afraid, Mrs Raynor. You have motor neurone disease.'

In a moment the landscape of our lives changed forever. Both into our seventies, with two sons and six grandchildren, we had been well positioned to enjoy whatever life had to offer. But suddenly the sunlit uplands had become overshadowed by rumbling storm clouds.

After a moment's stunned silence, I tried to bring some order to the chaos of thoughts and feelings churning inside me. Something like 'We're Christians, and we believe God can deal with this' was the best testimony I could manage in that moment. The doctor made no comment. He outlined the stark medical reality: no cure, no treatment. 'I can offer you one slight glimmer of light,' he said; 'this hospital has excellent support facilities for MND patients. You'll be under the care of Professor Young, who is one of the very best. And Professor Stephen Hawking lived with MND for fifty years.'

The last remark was well intended, but it didn't help Gwen, who had no desire to be confined to a wheelchair, unable to speak or live a normal life.

Some months earlier, Gwen had tripped in the street and landed heavily on her face and one hand, so much so that her glasses were broken. I asked the doctor if that could have been the trigger for motor neurone disease, but he said not. I have since heard of rugby players, much younger than Gwen, contracting the disease, and what they have in common, of course, is heavy body contact, sometimes involving a clash of heads. At the time of writing, I read that the incidence of motor neurone disease is four times greater among footballers than among the general population of the UK. Heading a football has been shown to lead to cases of dementia in later life. Might a bang on the head in a heavy fall possibly trigger motor neurone disease? Thus far, we do not know. Research is ongoing.

What MND does, to my mind, is rather like having a large room filled with interconnected computers, and gradually, one by one, the connections switch off and each computer stops functioning. A neuron is a specialised cell in the human body that transmits nerve impulses. Once that transmission is interrupted by the disease, that part of the body begins to shut down.

The immediate question I put to Gwen as we sat in the car in the hospital car park was this: 'Do you want to go to Bible Week, or do you want to go home?' We talked, and Gwen decided she was happy to go to Newark. We would not tell people about her diagnosis – that would have put a dampener on the week for our church friends. One exception: 'I want you to tell John and Julia,' said Gwen.

John and Julia Sutton-Smith were, like us, founder members of Southport Community Church, in May 1983. John was one of the initial two elders, and he and Julia were widely respected across the churches and in several nations as a wise, loving and godly couple. John had also been my colleague on the staff of Scarisbrick Hall School for nineteen years; during eleven of my twenty-one years as Headmaster, he had been my Deputy.

We were staying offsite in Newark, but among the tents and caravans inside the showground our church – like many others – had a marquee with tables, chairs, sofas, fridges, microwaves and cooking hobs. It served as a communal hub where campers and those from offsite could get together and – when necessary – shelter from the rain!

By the time we reached the Showground, most of our church's campers had set up, so there were quite a few folk in the marquee when we arrived. John and Julia were there, so I approached them and indicated that I had something to tell them, but without disclosing it to others. We stepped to one side of the marquee, and my emotions took over initially as I tried desperately to get the words out while at the same time hoping I wasn't attracting the attention of people around the marquee.

John has many good qualities, but one thing he has never mastered is the skill of whispering. On hearing my news, he immediately began to pray out loud. And yes, it was certainly loud enough for inquisitive ears to pick up, but as I looked round I could tell that through the hum of conversations nobody seemed to be listening to John's prayer. So far so good.

The only other person that I know had worked out Gwen's condition was another long-time friend, also a founder member of the Church, Maureen Stoddart. Her nurse training and wide experience led her to the right conclusion at the end of one of the evening meetings during Bible Week. An appeal had been made for those in need of healing to go forward for prayer. Maureen was sitting with us. I went with Gwen to the front of the meeting. It was Jim Harkins, a pastor from the USA, who came to lay hands on Gwen and pray for her. It was so noisy, with music playing and many people being prayed for, that Jim didn't ask us what the problem was, but he prayed in faith. We were both in tears as we returned to our seats. We confirmed to Maureen what she had guessed – that Gwen had been diagnosed with MND – and said only John and Julia knew, so please to keep it quiet for now. She wisely advised us to speak to our sons before we let other people know.

During the week, we both had tearful moments and also times when we affirmed what the Bible says about God's promises in relation to healing. I had a real sense of hope that God would heal her.

Out of the depths I cry to you, O Lord;
O Lord, hear my voice. [Psalm 130:1]

One verse that Gwen found particularly hard to deal with in the 28 months that followed was Romans 8: 28. She queried more than once how her having motor neurone disease could have anything good associated with it.

The various manuscripts which the translators have used give slightly different renderings of this verse. Generally accepted is either 'And we know that in all things God works for the good of those who love him, who have been called according to his purpose' or 'And we know that all things work together for good to those who love God …'

The context in this part of Romans 8 is prayer and the way in which the Holy Spirit works with believers to make prayer effective. He can use even our inarticulate sighs and groans to weave together something presentable at the throne of God. Healing is not specifically mentioned, but neither are any other specifics. Paul is saying that within the infinitely wide range of 'all things', the Spirit has the power to transform our feeble words and thoughts into effective prayer. Healing must come within that range.

The Greek uses 'panta' [=all things] 'sunergei' [work together], the latter word giving us the English 'synergy'. The inference to be drawn is that one element on its own cannot achieve what a synergy of several different components can bring about.

It was months after Gwen's passing away that I heard a helpful slant on this verse on a Christian radio station. To eat so many grams of flour on their own would not be beneficial; likewise to swallow some raw eggs would be unpleasant to most people. But combine flour, eggs and other ingredients according to a recipe and you could end up with a delicious cake. The items individually might do more harm than good, but together – combined in the right way by someone who knows what they are doing – those items can produce something really good.

I will explore this more, later in the book. For now suffice to say that we have personally witnessed miraculous healings and are convinced that signs and wonders are very much integral to the church's interaction with the world.

After returning home from Bible Week, it wasn't possible immediately to speak to our two sons about Gwen's diagnosis. Both boys are school teachers and it was now their summer holidays. One was away; the other had a daughter undergoing knee surgery.

One step I was able to take was to send an email to the church elders and the worship team leader to say that for an indeterminate period I would need to be out of frontline duties such as preaching and singing. I did not specify why, but told them I would be more forthcoming as soon as possible. At that stage I wasn't sure I could look a congregation in the face and declare or sing about the goodness of God without breaking down in tears.

2. Sympathy or compassion?

IT WAS TEN days after Bible Week when I was finally able to talk to our church elders, Geoff Grice and Dave Gregg. As I walked into Geoff's office I said, 'Please don't be nice to me!' They understood that a gentle, sympathetic approach was guaranteed to bring tears. What we needed was compassion, not sympathy.

Sympathy says: 'Ah, poor you. I'm really sorry.' Usually with a sad face and a stare into your eyes. Some nurses, as well as concerned friends, genuinely believe that this is the right way to cope with a terminal diagnosis. They want you to know they care – the modern word is 'empathise'. But it tends to reinforce the condition rather than alleviate it. It forces the sufferer to stay within the shackles of the condition, rather than giving them a way through.

Compassion is different. Compassion says: 'What can I do to help you?' Jesus was often 'moved with compassion': I take that to mean that his loving nature moved him to look for answers to people's needs. And whenever the gospel narrative includes that phrase, it is always a prelude to a miracle. Gwen needed compassion: she needed a miracle.

When I gave Geoff and Dave the facts, they of course expressed love, concern and support; they prayed; and they assured me of being available at any time to help us in whatever way they could. Immediately after I left them, and unbeknown to me, they emailed all our church leaders with the news. The following day, they passed the message on to all church members, although they must have deliberately not sent it to Gwen or me.

Consequently, I was a wee bit bemused at a Prayer and Praise gathering the following evening, when prayer was requested for various people's health needs and Gwen wasn't mentioned. I assumed that the elders were waiting for the Sunday morning meeting to announce it to the church. So, some time between Wednesday evening and Sunday morning, I sent an email to Amanda Carr, our church's administrator, asking her to forward it to church members. At that point Dave messaged me to let me know that they had already circulated the news of Gwen's diagnosis. And it wasn't just to our own folk: leaders of related churches across the UK and around the world, plus ministries and missionaries in many countries were alerted to pray for Gwen.

On the first Sunday after Bible Week, Gwen didn't fancy being seen by well-meaning church folk, so I went on my own to the meeting. The following week, however, Gwen decided she would come with me. Normally, if I am in the congregation, I like to sit at or near the front, but Gwen always preferred to be less conspicuous. I was happy to let her choose where to sit, so we occupied end seats about two thirds of the way back. I was on the outside seat to act as a human buffer, whilst also watching for flanking movements from along the row on the other side of Gwen.

One lady, Jan, who co-leads our Healing Rooms ministry with her husband, came to talk to us. Gwen quite happily listened and asked the odd question about Jan's family. Jan is softly-spoken, and even with my hearing aids I can't always tell what she is saying. Part of me would happily have gone to talk to someone else, as Gwen seemed comfortable, but when she sensed that I might be on the move, she quickly put her hand on my arm to make sure that her left flank remained well defended. At the end of the meeting, it was from Gwen's right flank that a down-to-earth lady called Tina approached. 'What's all this, then? Well, we're not 'avin' that!' she declared, briefly prayed, and left us. Gwen could cope with an approach like that. What she hated was the 'Ah-poor-you' approach and the doleful stare into her eyes.

3. Breaking it to the boys

TELLING OUR BOYS, Tim and John, about their mum's condition could have been quite emotional, but in neither case was it. I grew up in a loving family, as did Gwen, but neither of us remembered loving embraces or any encouragement to talk about our feelings as we grew up. I suppose something of that stoicism had rubbed off on our boys.

On the Saturday after Bible Week, John, our younger son, came with his wife Debs and their three girls for lunch, after which we went to one of the two very pleasant public parks in our area of Southport. Gwen had seen in the local press that the observatory in Hesketh Park would be open to the public, so it was a good time to go. All of us were intrigued by the orrery - a model of the planets in our solar system in relation to the sun - and the volunteers made our visit very interesting.

Afterwards, the girls were happily enjoying the busy play area, and John and I were standing to one side, watching them. The fact that we were not facing each other was probably very helpful, as I was able to broach the subject of Gwen's condition and give him the facts, as relayed to us by the doctors. With no eye contact between us, as our eyes were directed towards the children, any possible emotional response was averted. I heard some time later that when John relayed the information to Debs and the girls, there were tears all round. And all quite natural.

Three days later, Tim and Katie had brought Chloe, their middle child, home from her knee operation. Gwen was keen to see Chloe, as well as the rest of the family, at their home in Penwortham, a suburb of Preston. It's a twenty-five minute drive from our house to theirs.

Tim had arranged to drive a few miles to pick up the pieces of a double-glazed window unit, which he was going to use to replace their decaying kitchen window frame. If their eldest, Jonathan, had been at home, he would have gone with his dad to help, but I was happy to be a substitute and keep Tim company. I saw it as the ideal opportunity to tell him about Gwen's diagnosis. During the ten-minute drive I gave him the facts, and again, as we were sitting side by side in his car, there was no eye contact and no show of emotion. Later, he too would be in tears as he told Katie and the children.

Tears fascinate me. As the convention of the stiff upper lip has receded into the background in recent decades, it has been widely recognised that in times of trauma and tragedy it is not only good but necessary to let the tears flow. Without making any conscious resolve in that regard, I am aware that I have shed more tears in my seventies than probably the rest of my adult life put together. Confronted by the image of my favourite lady in the whole world with a death sentence over her, I was unashamed to let the tears flow as her condition deteriorated. Usually, I cried out of her sight, just after a session of intense focus on her needs. I don't remember Gwen crying very much at all, although perhaps she kept her tears for when I wasn't with her.

In the months after she had passed away, I was surprised that I didn't cry very often. Certainly there were times when I was just starting to share something with her and remembered she wasn't there; that really did hurt. But when I did allow the tears to flow, I sensed always that God was not wanting me to wallow: that would have been self-pity. Instead, I felt a strong sense of relief that her days of being constricted by the merciless MND were now over and she would be enjoying to the full the delights of eternal life with all those who have gone before, and principally with Jesus himself. The words of Psalm 16: 11 resonated strongly with me, as I was convinced that Gwen could identify 100% with what they said: 'You have made known to me the path of life; you will fill me with joy in your presence, with eternal pleasures at your right hand.'

4. To the wider family

AFTER I HAD told our sons about Gwen's diagnosis, I sent emails to other family members. In response, my brother Paul offered to come over the next day, but I said it really wasn't necessary. Gwen and I both wanted to live as normal a life as possible for as long as possible, without being forced to contemplate what could be a sad future.

One of the couples from church gave us a little booklet: 'God's Creative Power for Healing' by Charles Capps. (I was surprised later to find that we already had a copy in the house, but when or by whom it came to be there I do not know.) The thrust of the booklet is that Christians can release God's healing power into their bodies by speaking God's promises to their bodies. The writer recommends using God's word as an actual medicine, three times a day initially, until faith comes and then once a day. 'If circumstances grow worse, double the dosage. There are no harmful side effects.'

He uses paraphrases rather than direct quotations from the Bible, but does give biblical chapters and verses as a back-up. So, for example: 'Jesus bore my sickness and carried my pain. Therefore I give no place to sickness or pain. For God sent his word and healed me.' [Psalm

107:20] And: 'You have given me abundant life. I receive that life through your word and it flows to every organ of my body bringing healing and health.' [John 10:10; John 6:63]

Gwen and I had no qualms about declaring the truths of God's word and the promises of healing contained in the Bible.

Meanwhile, Gwen had taken a phone call from her sister-in-law, Norma, and there were tears at both ends of the line as she outlined the facts. Norma and David, Gwen's brother, came to Southport not long afterwards, as did my brother Paul and his wife, Pat. Both occasions caused no emotional problems, as we all shared the belief that – cliché or not – life goes on, and we must take one day at a time. It was important to focus on what we ***could*** do, rather than get caught up with a tangle of negative thoughts and attitudes. We had always encouraged our boys and others to have an attitude of gratitude, and now that was no platitude! We had so many blessings and so many things that we were able to do, so it was no hardship to thank God regularly and often throughout the next 28 months. I believe that approach in itself is therapeutic.

I have set the Lord always before me. Because he is at my right hand, I will not be shaken. [Psalm 16:8]

On the third Sunday after Bible Week, Gwen was scheduled to be one of the welcomers in the church porch, and she readily carried out that responsibility and was able to stay after the meeting for coffee and fellowship.

5. Over to the experts

THURSDAY 16TH **AUGUST 2018** was the date of Gwen's appointment with Dr Young. We had tickets for Southport Flower Show and had intended to use them on that day, but they were valid for the following three days as well, so we altered our plans.

The Sid Watkins Building is part of the complex that comprises the Aintree University Hospital in Liverpool. We met with kindness as soon as we arrived in the car park, as a man who was leaving gave us his part-used ticket, giving us two hours' free parking.

Two nurses checked Gwen's height, weight, body mass index [BMI], blood pressure, breath flow and oxygen level. Then we met Professor Young, who turned out to be a lady. Her main concern was Gwen's BMI, which was far too low at 18. Gwen's dilemma had been that she had previously been diagnosed as having type 2 diabetes, so she had been careful about what she ate and had lost some weight. The professor told her to ignore the diabetes, as MND was far more serious. Gwen needed to put on weight, which would improve muscle support, stamina and energy.

Gwen's speech was already a little slurred, though still totally comprehensible, but because the brand of MND that she had was bulbar, it would affect every muscle in her mouth and throat, as well as reducing muscular power generally. When a speech therapist showed us a tablet with a voice app, Gwen became quite upset at the projected loss of speech. She didn't want her young grandchildren to be upset by Grandma's strange way of talking. I assured her that youngsters quickly adapt to things like that. In the event, when we were loaned one of these tablets by the MND Association, the grandchildren made a game out of typing in words for the artificial voice to speak.

Gwen's response during the appointment was to point a pretend gun with her fingers at her head: she didn't want to prolong what she knew would be a difficult journey. Professor Young said she had patients who lived for ten years with this type of motor neurone disease, although she could never guarantee that Gwen would have that long.

> *The cords of death entangled me; the torrents of destruction overwhelmed me. The cords of the grave coiled around me; the snares of death confronted me. [Psalm 18:4-5]*

There was, apparently, a drug – riluzole - that was not readily available in pharmacies, but it could be prescribed for Gwen if she wanted it. We asked what it would do and whether there were side effects. We were amazed when the professor said, completely straight-faced, that it could extend life by up to two months. Two months? I didn't quote John McEnroe's 'You cannot be serious!' although I was tempted.

One side effect of this drug was the likelihood of vomiting. Now Gwen had always had a hatred of vomiting, so that just underlined the negative response we gave to the offer of riluzole. 'You can always change your mind later if you decide you would like to try it,' said the professor. We both knew that was never going to happen.

I suppose that if you regard this human existence as all there is in the grand scheme of things, then a possible two-month extension might seem an attractive proposition. For us, however, there has always been the deep conviction that there is a God and there is an after-life and that those who live this life with God at the centre will find that death is merely a curtain of access into a richer and fuller life beyond. Why try to add on two months of limited existence when there was the prospect of freedom and glory after all this? Even if this drug could have added five years to Gwen's life span, I don't think we would have accepted it, because it would prolong the process by which MND was going to restrict and constrict her quality of life. Unless God intervened and healed her….

6. The God who heals

ON SEPTEMBER 18TH 2018 my daily Bible reading included these words: 'As for you, I'll come with healing, curing the incurable.' That is Jeremiah 30: 17 in *The Message*. I know that this version is a paraphrase rather than a close translation. I also know that I should not take a scripture out of its context and use it to suit my own circumstances. Nevertheless, I do believe, as a principle of my faith, that God is perfectly capable of curing the incurable. I know that raises questions such as 'If God can cure the incurable, why doesn't he just cure every illness at a stroke and make the world a happier place?' For now, I will have to leave that question hanging in the air.

What I can say, from personal experience as well as Biblical teaching, is that God heals people today, just as he did when Jesus walked the earth. On three specific occasions, in response to prayers of faith in Jesus Christ, I have been healed.

The first occasion was over twenty years ago. I was preaching in the Community Church one Sunday morning when I sensed the Holy Spirit telling me to pause and throw out a particular challenge. I said, 'Excuse me for a moment; I'll pick up the thread of what I'm saying in a moment. God has told me to issue this challenge. From time to time I have bad pain in my elbow, and God wants someone here who has never prayed for healing to come to me after the meeting and do just that.' Then I carried on with what I had been saying previously.

After the meeting I stayed at the front and within a few seconds a young lady called Karen Barnes came to me and said, 'David, it's me. God prompted me to pray for your healing.' I grinned at her, because she came across as being a little nervous; she was certainly not a person who enjoyed being the centre of attention. I honestly can't remember whether other people were even aware that Karen was responding to the challenge, as the meeting had finished and people were talking and moving about. Anyway, I indicated to Karen which elbow had the problem, whereupon she laid her hands on it and prayed aloud, briefly and directly, for healing.

I told her that the elbow hadn't been sore that morning, so I couldn't give her an immediate response as to the healing, but both Karen and I were content to leave the outcome to God. In the weeks that followed, I was able to tell Karen that I had had no more pain in the elbow. Weeks became months and then years, and the elbow has not had any pain at all. Not the slightest twinge – ever. It has been a joy on more than one occasion to tell the church that Karen's prayer had the desired effect and that healing has stayed with me. Karen actually went on to become a valued member of the Healing Rooms ministry which the church runs.

My second experience of healing took place when I was serving on the Healing Rooms team. I had several times experienced itching inside my ears; it was diagnosed as eczema. To relieve the irritation I used to insert a finger in the itchy ear and wiggle it about. What then tended to happen was that some time afterwards I would suffer two things: my hearing became blocked and an intense pain would follow. My GP had made a particular study of things ear-related, so I went to see him with confidence that he would sort me out. He explained that when I put my finger in my ear, I was introducing bacteria that became lodged inside, causing infection and the resulting pain. A week's antibiotics would clear the infection, then he would use a special instrument he had perfected to remove the gunge that had clogged up the inner ear. I learnt the lesson not to stick my finger inside my ear, for any reason.

One Saturday morning, during a lull in proceedings at Healing Rooms, I mentioned to Ben and Maureen McMaster, the leaders, that I occasionally suffered from eczema in the ears and if they would pray for healing, I would be very grateful. They gladly laid hands on me, prayed simple affirmative prayers and that was that. I told them I didn't have the eczema at the time, so I couldn't give immediate evidence of healing, but we all said with confident expectation that I was healed. I am pleased to report that, perhaps fifteen years later, the eczema has never returned.

When serving in Healing Rooms, we learnt that many healings take time and patient persistence. We would all like to see the immediate, obvious, dramatic healings, and we have seen some of those. Generally, though, healing has not been instantaneous.

One dramatic healing that brought joy and excitement when it was reported concerned a young woman who came because her hearing was defective. She had applied to join the police, but the tests she had had to undergo included one for hearing, and the printout she showed us of the graph of her results was conclusive. Her hearing was well below the standard required.

A week after the team had prayed for her, she returned. The look on her face suggested something amazing had happened. The new printout of her test results showed a line right across the top of the columns. What a difference! Praise God! It's always good to have medical confirmation of a miracle. The young woman was absolutely delighted; she could now pursue the career she had set her heart on.

The third occasion when I know I was healed came in more recent times, when I was in my mid-seventies. People tend to assume that at that stage of life it is only natural for aches and pains to increase, with arthritis probably the major culprit. Others would contend that God created us in his image to live in health, whatever our age. And the thought that follows on from that: Everyone's preferred way to die would be to go to sleep one night and not to wake up in the morning, some time when we are 'old, and full of days'.

I suffered from pain in my left wrist, specifically at the base of my thumb, and when the doctor sent me to see a physiotherapist at the local hospital, that lady said it was osteo-arthritis. Anti-inflammatories might help, but there wasn't really a cure. It wasn't painful all the time, so I learned to live with it for perhaps a couple of years. I didn't bother with anti-inflammatories.

But then I had an upsurge of more constant pain in both wrists. I would be sitting at home doing something on my iPad, and I would suddenly gasp as pain shot through my wrist. I would apologise to Gwen for startling her. This happened increasingly. I like to play the occasional game of golf, and my sons were keen to have a game, but when I picked up a golf club, there was no way that I could begin to do even a practice swing without severe pain. Just to grip the club in two hands was agony.

At this point I have to confess to being one of God's slow learners. It can take a long time for a biblical truth, which may have been so obvious to others, to sink in. I realised that, although I have quoted the following scripture to other people on several occasions, I had not in fact applied it to myself. It's a bit like the stories you hear of ministers who preach the gospel so powerfully that they themselves come under conviction and open their hearts fully to God, perhaps for the first time.

James 5: 14 - 15 says this: 'Is any of you sick? He should call the elders of the church to pray over him and anoint him with oil in the name of the Lord. And the prayer offered in faith will make the sick person well; the Lord will raise him up.' That's pretty straightforward, really.

It was at the end of a Sunday church meeting that I was in conversation with Geoff, one of our two elders, and my wrist pain was mentioned. Happily, the penny dropped quickly enough for me to say, 'I think I ought to do things the Bible way and ask the church elders to anoint me with oil and pray for healing.'

'We'll do it now,' said Geoff, as he looked around for Dave, the other elder. When Dave came across in response to Geoff's call and the reason was explained, Dave grinned as he brought the bottle of oil we have at the front of the church building. 'It's in my interests for David to be healed, so we can play golf together.' Apart from my sons, Dave is the man with whom I have played golf most often over the years. Geoff has tried golf in the past, but he is now firmly in the company of those who say that golf is a good walk spoiled; or, as he points out, 'golf' is 'flog' spelt backwards.

They applied the oil to my hands and forehead, and prayed in the name of Jesus; I thanked them and went home.

A week later, I was able to tell them I had not experienced any pain in either wrist.

Six weeks later, still no pain.

Three months later, I played golf with Dave and my two sons. NO PAIN! Praise God!

> *Praise the Lord, O my soul, and forget not all his benefits – who forgives all your sins and heals all your diseases ...*

7. John Wimber at Wembley

MY FIRST DIRECT involvement in a healing miracle involved a loss of hearing: it took place at the Wembley Conference Centre in October 1985. My friends John and Julia had heard that John Wimber was having a week of meetings there, and that week coincided with our half-term break. John's sister and brother-in-law lived in Hertfordshire, just north of Greater London, so they accommodated us and also came to the meetings.

John Wimber had already established a wide reputation as a 'healing evangelist'. He had been a professional musician, working with the Righteous Brothers in the 1960s and 70s. When he became a Christian, he went to a church meeting; when it finished he asked, 'So when do we get to do the stuff?' 'What stuff do you mean?' they asked. 'The stuff that they did in Acts when the church was born: healings, miracles, signs and wonders.' That was not to be the last occasion on which he put the charismatic cat among the religious pigeons!

Seeing John Wimber at Wembley impressed me – not by any Hollywood-style presentation, but through his down-to-earth humility. He strongly believed in the power of praise and worship to create a platform for the Holy

Spirit to work from, so after we had sung and clapped and shouted and praised and knelt and danced, he would walk up and down along the front of the platform and just chat to the congregation. 'I'm just a little fat guy trying to get to heaven' was one line that stuck in the memory. Then at some point he would say, 'OK, let's have some fun.' (No prizes for guessing why some traditional, 'mainstream' churches would have nothing to do with Wimber.) He would pray a simple prayer, inviting the Holy Spirit to begin to move in the gathering. He was very open: 'I don't know what's going to happen, but we need to give God room to manoeuvre.'

And then he would give a running commentary as ripples passed through the gathering. Someone might begin to sway, or someone's hands begin to tremble, or someone would start chuckling or sobbing. He would draw attention to what the Spirit seemed to be doing without ever making the individuals become self-conscious. He pointed out that the surface sign wasn't the essence; it was more like a symptom of what was going on inside the person.

So it was that in a particular meeting that week, he invited people to stand if they needed healing. He usually had words of knowledge so that he could specify which conditions the Spirit was wanting to deal with. On this occasion it was people with hearing problems. Sometimes he would call them down to the front of the meeting so that he and his team could lay hands on people and pray, but this time he invited us all to look round to see where people were standing and he told us that we were going to do the ministry.

Just behind me and to my right was a lady, perhaps in her fifties, standing with hands spread above her waist as if to receive from God. She said she was completely deaf in her right ear, so I put my left hand to her right ear. Other people came around as well and we prayed. Within about twenty seconds, tears began to trickle from her closed eyes, her face lit up, then she opened her eyes and said, 'I can hear perfectly!' As we rejoiced with her, she quietly said thank you to me for placing my hand on her ear, as she felt that was the key to her healing.

> *And these signs will accompany those who believe: … they will place their hands on sick people, and they will get well. [Mark 16:17-18]*

That memory is still so strong that if ever I have any doubts about God healing people, I can quickly go back in my mind to Wembley, October 1985.

8. Help from the medics

ABOUT A MONTH after Gwen's visit to see Professor Young at Aintree hospital, she was experiencing pain in her ribs. I rang to get her an appointment with our GP, Dr Tobin. He reassured her that the pain was muscular and unrelated to MND. He said he had no experience of riluzole, so he could not advise us about it. What he did say was that Gwen should stop taking metformin for the diabetes, as she needed to put on weight. That was the same message as Professor Young had given us.

Dr Tobin put Gwen on the practice's 'gold list', which gave immediate access or priority at any time to his services. He also expressed his concern for my wellbeing, impressing me to the point where I followed Gwen's lead with a few tears. Any time I wanted to talk to him, he would be available.

In October we had a first visit from Rachel, a speech and language therapist. Drinking from a cup was becoming difficult for Gwen, so Rachel proposed various solutions. One was to try a thickener, adding powder to a drink to make it easier to take on board. Gwen did try this, but she hated the feel of the drink – the texture put her off completely.

Another possibility was a different kind of drinking vessel: a cup with a spout, or a baby-style mouthpiece.

Gwen's problem was that her lips had lost all sensation, so she was unable to pucker them into a shape that would contain any kind of mouthpiece, let alone the rim of a cup or mug. A straw was even more frustrating: her lips could not grip that either. She persevered with an ordinary mug for some time, using a saucer underneath it to catch the increasing amount of dribble that emerged from the attempt at drinking.

Two contrasting conditions became a major cause for Gwen's concern: her mouth felt dry constantly, yet at the same time she was dribbling saliva. Tissues, paper towels, kitchen roll, all became her constant companions.

Rachel had to broach the topic of longer term intake of nourishment. If Gwen could not drink or chew or swallow, at some point, they would have to think about feeding her via a tube, either down her throat or directly into her stomach. Gwen was horrified and tearful.

She coped a little better with a televised interview that came on the BBC's 'The One Show'. Doddie Weir had been a Scotland international rugby player and had toured with the British and Irish Lions. He was 6 feet 5 inches tall [1.96 metres], and built like a wardrobe. And now he was suffering from motor neurone disease. He was a jovial character, widely loved across the rugby-playing nations, and he was using his status and contacts as a rugby international to raise funds for research into the disease.

When I saw that he was going to be interviewed, I warned Gwen that she might be upset, but she wanted to see the programme. Doddie's brand of MND was different from hers, so his speech was still good: he was losing power in his legs at that point, but was still working as much as he could manage on his farm.

On November 8th 2018 Gwen had a sore mouth, so I rang to make an appointment with Dr Tobin. Having prescribed medication, he went on to ask whether we had talked about places we wanted to visit or things we wanted to do together. Not the most subtle hint that Gwen's time here would be limited, but realistic. Gwen immediately picked up on the direction the conversation had taken, so she asked whether he was thinking about palliative care and linking her up with the hospice. He said that patients usually left it late to ask for palliative care, but the practice could call on two palliative nurses who could visit patients at home. It might be wise to make that contact sooner rather than later. With our permission he would take that step on our behalf.

I think I was more upset than Gwen at this point. The doctor's words seemed to place the sword of Damocles very clearly above Gwen's head. From now on, if things progressed as the medics expected, she was on death row.

My Bible reading the following day included these verses from Psalm 107: 18ff:-

'... and they were knocking on death's door. "Lord, help!" they cried in their trouble, and he saved them from their distress. He sent out his word and healed them, snatching them from the door of death. Let them praise the Lord for his great love and for the wonderful things he has done for them.'

The psalmist is thinking about people generally, rather than specific instances; people have known what it is to be having a hard time and to call out to God, and he has come to the rescue. There is nothing to suggest that our circumstances could not be covered by the same God acting in the same way. Yet we know that many people die, even after a massive prayer effort by their friends and churches.

The Bible presents us with images of God's ultimate Kingdom rule, when pain, illness, persecution and death will be at an end. It is a wonderful prospect. In the meantime, we are encouraged to grasp the reality that God's Kingdom is already with us in a measure. Some preachers talk of the Kingdom 'now and not yet' or of drawing the future down into the present. That being so, we have every incentive to expect and to pray for signs, wonders and miracles in this present age. Only God knows where the boundaries are and why some are healed miraculously and others are not. Therefore, to quote John Wimber again, 'If I pray for nineteen people in succession and none of them is healed, I'm still going to pray for Number 20 to be healed!'

Jesus himself accepted the fact that accidents and disasters happen to people, irrespective of their moral status. Christians are not immune to the 'slings and arrows of outrageous fortune' that oppressed the mind of Shakespeare's Hamlet. In Luke 13: 1-5, Jesus draws a salutary lesson from the misfortunes of two groups of people: 'Now there were some present at that time who told Jesus about the Galileans whose blood Pilate had mixed with their sacrifices. Jesus answered, "Do you think that these Galileans were worse sinners than all the other Galileans because they suffered in this way? I tell you, no! But unless you repent, you too will all perish. Or those eighteen who died when the tower in Siloam fell on them – do you think they were more guilty than all the others living in Jerusalem? I tell you, no! But unless you repent, you too will all perish."'

The day after we had been confronted with our GP's gloomy expectation, we had a visit from the team leader of the palliative nurses at the Hospice. Cathy was very professional, asking lots of questions about details of Gwen's condition; Gwen found it hard at times. In summing up, Cathy said we would qualify for attendance allowance and she would set the process in motion that would, as it turned out, provide us with £80+ per week! She also said that Gwen would qualify for a blue parking badge, if we wanted it. We declined at that stage, believing that Gwen's mobility and walking were certainly good enough for a while yet. Presumably Cathy was expecting Gwen's strength and stamina to decline as the months passed. And yes, that did happen, though not just then.

9. An enjoyable interlude

IN EARLY DECEMBER 2018 on a bright, crisp morning, Gwen fancied a trip out in the car to Rivington. It's about a 45-minute drive from our house: as you go east from Southport towards the Pennines, you come first to a hilly area that includes Winter Hill and Rivington Pike. It's a bit fiddly to get there, as the major roads all go from north to south and we were heading west to east. At ground level there are acres of woodland to walk through, and Rivington Barn houses a very popular café and bar. We planned to go for a walk in the woods and then have something to eat.

It was sunny but cold. I had taken a cap and a woolly hat, but on leaving the car in the Barn car park, I realised it was a woolly hat day, so I left the cap in the car. Gwen was clearly being stimulated by the cold air, because she suddenly suggested that we head towards the Pike. 'We can always turn back if it gets too much for us,' she said. I happily agreed, but I took the precaution of going back to the car for my cap, as Gwen didn't have any headgear and could wear my woolly hat. Once we went above the tree-line, as we might eventually do, we would be exposed to the wind as well as frosty air.

I was happy for Gwen to set the pace, and she amazed me. I was the one struggling with the cold air after about ten minutes [being slightly asthmatic], whereas Gwen just kept walking determinedly forward. Rivington Pike stands just under 1,200 feet [366 metres] above sea level and as we came out of the final stretch of trees we could see the summit ahead and above us. Some walkers were coming down, so we asked whether it was worth the effort to reach the top. They convinced us that you could see for miles from the top – the Jodrell Bank radio telescope, the Isle of Man, the Lake District.

So on we went up the long, gentle slope. The last hundred feet or so [33 metres] were steeper, but we made it. Using the tower on top as a windbreak, we looked all round at the view and were glad we had done it, both feeling quite exhilarated.

> *I lift up my eyes to the hills – where does my help come from? My help comes from the Lord, the Maker of heaven and earth. [Psalm 121: 1-2]*

We decided to try a different downward route and found that there was work going on in various places that were cordoned off. There used to be ornate gardens on the side of the hill and they were in process of being restored. So we had to zigzag down some steep stretches, but at least there were clear, safe paths.

We were about a third of the way down when my mobile phone rang. It was Rachel Barry, the speech and language therapist calling to ask how Gwen was. She laughed incredulously when I told her that Gwen and I were on our way down from the summit of Rivington Pike. I think Gwen went several notches higher in Rachel's esteem.

It was the end of January 2019 when Rachel came to the house again. She said she couldn't detect much change from her previous visit. That was the kind of minimal good news that was intended to cheer Gwen up, but deep down she saw it rather as prolonging the inevitable. Rachel talked about an app which Gwen could use as a voice simulator when her speech deteriorated. The Motor Neurone Disease Association provides iPads for MND patients to be able to use this app. We thought at the time that we didn't want to put the charity to that expense, not realising that the iPad would be on loan, not a gift. So Rachel said she would order an iPad for Gwen to use.

Early in February, my Bible reading included these words from Hosea chapter 2:15:-

> *'I will lead her into the desert and speak tenderly to her. There I will give her back her vineyards, and will make the Valley of Achor [= Trouble] a door of hope. Then she will sing as in the days of her youth...'*

It was the singing bit that first resonated with me; I felt that God was saying Gwen's gradual loss of vocal strength would be reversed and that she would sing again. Gwen had sung with the Songsters for many years at the Salvation Army, and during our married life she had been part of inter-church choirs that performed at the Liverpool Philharmonic Hall and at the Royal Albert Hall in London.

But there was also the bit about making the Valley of Trouble a door of hope. I wrote these words out and stuck them in the centre of my desk so that I would have them in front of me every time I was there, for studying, praying or writing.

I shared the verses with our Connect Group, which met on a Monday morning, and asked them to use them when praying for Gwen. The church's two elders, Geoff and Dave, came after that Group meeting, at my request, to anoint Gwen with oil and to pray for healing. To follow the Bible's instructions is always a good thing to do, whatever the outcome.

When Rachel Barry came to show us how to use the app on the iPad, we thought it might be useful, although in the event, it turned out to be something to amuse grandchildren rather than a useful tool for Gwen, who preferred to write things down when she could no longer speak.

10. Help from the hospice

AT THE END of June 2019 we had a visit from Angela McKenna, who had replaced the now retired Cathy Brownley as senior palliative nurse at the Hospice. She asked plenty of getting-to-know-you questions, some of which brought tears. Angela said she would arrange for Gwen to see a psychologist at the Hospice. As Gwen was having difficulty cutting her toenails – and didn't particularly trust me not to nick the flesh of her toes! – Angela also said she would set up an appointment for Gwen to see a podiatrist.

She asked how Gwen would feel about having a PEG – a tube inserted in the stomach so that I could feed her directly; Gwen was by now struggling with any mouth actions – sucking, biting, swallowing, chewing. Angela said that the stomach shrinks and we require less food as we lose weight. Gwen wasn't keen on having a tube in her tummy. She also said that she would like to die in the Hospice – not at home and not in hospital. Angela said that might not be possible, as they have only ten beds at Queenscourt.

Throughout this time, our church friends were regularly praying for Gwen's healing and I remained certain that

God could heal her at any time. Gwen knew that to be true, but she was facing up more realistically to the possibility of her dying sooner rather than later. She insisted she didn't want to end up like Professor Stephen Hawking, in a wheelchair for fifty years and totally dependent on others for 'normal' living. She did talk about Dignitas, the Swiss clinic to which people go for 'assisted dying' at £10,000 a time. She contemplated that way out, partly to shorten the expected horrors of the death process, but mainly to save me from having to devote so much time and attention to her needs. She perhaps felt free to speak about Dignitas because she knew that I would never agree to it in any circumstances.

> *No man has power over the wind to contain it;*
> *so no one has power over the day of his death.*
> *[Ecclesiastes 8:8]*

> *...Man is destined to die once, and after that to face judgement ... [Hebrews 9:27]*

My view has always been that God gives us life and it is for him to take it from us at his appointed time. I hear the arguments for euthanasia and the safeguards that would be attached to any legislation for assisted dying, but I hear also the testimonies of people in horrendously painful situations who maintain that the dignity of human life is sacrosanct. My own experience of the hospice movement also convinces me that our government should increase the funding of palliative care through hospices rather than legislate to allow people to take a human life, whether their own or someone else's.

In mid-July 2019 Gwen had an appointment with Dr Dominic Bray, a psychologist. His approach was gentle, thoughtful, never hurried, quietly eliciting the information he needed about Gwen's mental state. Understandably, again, some of the questions led to tears. But her eyes brightened and her attitude perked up when she realised who Dr Bray was married to. He had talked, early in the conversation, about our Christian faith and our church life, and he eventually revealed that he was a member of St Philip's and St Paul's with Wesley Church, a combined Anglican-Methodist congregation with premises just around the corner from our own. In fact, the Methodists were the original owners of the buildings that our church now occupies, and it was only when their numbers were in serious decline that they sold up and moved round the corner.

In 2017 a 'Good News Choir' had been brought together from Christians across the Southport churches to put on a musical based on the Good News Bible. Gwen had enjoyed singing in that choir, particularly as it was so ably led and conducted by Dr Bray's wife.

August 19th 2019 was our first meeting with Dr Clare Finegan at Queenscourt Hospice. It turned out that she knew our daughter-in-law, Debs, as she has children similar in age to our grandchildren. I think they both had a child attending the same pre-school nursery.

Our principal concern was Gwen's breathing, which had become quite laboured in recent weeks. Dr Tobin, our GP, had told Gwen to use her inhaler as often as she needed it, not to limit herself to so many puffs a day. Dr Finegan said she would set up appointments with various therapists at the Hospice, each of whom could make a contribution to easing Gwen's breathing problems. She would also refer Gwen to the respiratory team at the Walton Centre in Aintree Hospital.

Tricia Biddolph was the occupational therapist. She suggested a variety of ways to deal with practical problems. For example, as Gwen lost the power to grip, with her left hand in particular, she had a gadget to attach to the tap at the kitchen sink and another one for opening jars.

Imogen Baddeley was the physiotherapist and showed Gwen how to improve her breathing, using various techniques and exercises.

Jane Boulton's title was a complementary therapist, which didn't mean much to us until she explained that she focused on ways to help Gwen reduce stress, be more relaxed and therefore also help her with her breathing.

Gwen responded very positively to the suggestion of massages.

All three women were brisk and businesslike, always looking for positive ways to help Gwen.

11. Hospital procedures

AT OUR FIRST appointment with Professor Young at Aintree, she had said that she would see Gwen again in six months. In reality it was a full twelve months – August 29th 2019 – before that second appointment.

The professor immediately expressed concern about Gwen's weight loss. Eating had become so difficult, as the muscles in lips, mouth and tongue closed down. Our friend Maureen had lent us a blender, so that whatever evening meal I was having could be at least partly liquidised and Gwen could manage to swallow it. Nevertheless, she now weighed only seven stone [44 kilos].

Professor Young said she would get Dr Tobin to prescribe supplements, but she again mentioned the value of having a feeding tube inserted into the stomach. She was very positive and reassuring, setting Gwen's concerns at rest. To fit the tube would require only a local anaesthetic, so she would not need to stay overnight in the hospital. And she would decide when to use the tube and how often, although they would give her guidance.

Gwen was quite blunt at one point: 'Isn't all this just prolonging the agony of dying?' To which the professor replied calmly that they were always looking to see how they could improve the quality of patients' lives.

To measure Gwen's breathlessness, the professor said she could use an oximeter. This involves having a little clamp on the finger attached to a small machine which measures the amount of oxygen in the blood. Wearing that through the night would not affect her sleep at all, but would help them to assess the level of her breathing. The only downside was that the oximeter had to be returned to the sleep clinic before 11 a.m. the next day. Oh joy! Another 36-mile round trip for me, with the everlasting doubt about parking spaces.

September 12th 2019 found us again at Aintree, this time in the Neuromuscular department with Dr Chakrabati. Lots of questions about sleeping and breathing in particular. The doctor felt it would be advisable to have Gwen in the hospital for a few days so that both aspects could be monitored.

On the way home, Gwen said she was happy enough about the mechanics of fitting and using a feeding tube, but she really didn't want it to be simply a way of prolonging her life if, for example, she ended up paralysed. I was so impressed that she was facing up to the likelihood of death and was very calm at the prospect. That is testimony to the depth and assurance of her faith in God, that she was not clinging desperately to life on this earth, convinced as she was that there is a far better life beyond that moment of death for those who have committed their lives to Jesus Christ.

> *No, in all these things we are more than conquerors through him who loved us. For I am convinced that neither death nor life, neither angels nor demons, neither the present nor the future, nor any powers, neither height nor depth, nor anything else in all creation, will be able to separate us from the love of God that is in Christ Jesus our Lord.* [Romans 8: 37-39]

A week later we were with a podiatrist in the Churchtown clinic. The hospice nurse had kindly set up an appointment, as Gwen's loss of grip in her hands made it too difficult for her to trim her toenails. She was wise not to entrust the job to me, as I could not guarantee that I would avoid nicking a sliver of flesh as well as a nail! The podiatrist asked a lot of questions, checked that the pulses in Gwen's feet were in good order, then gave the nails a good trim, as well as rubbing the soles of her feet with a file. We were to book another appointment in about ten weeks' time.

Gwen's date for a 48-hour admission to Aintree hospital had been set for October 10th, but on the 1st of the month we had a phone call to say that a bed was available if Gwen wanted to have it and we could be there within a couple of hours. I was quite surprised that Gwen immediately said Yes, so I gladly took her.

The VIC (Ventilation Inpatient Clinic) is a spacious area on the first floor of Aintree hospital, just above the main entrance. Gwen was admitted to a large, pleasant, ensuite room with a view over the front of the hospital grounds. It would not be possible to fit the feeding tube on this visit – as had been the plan – as the requisite doctor was away.

While I was there, we had tutorials in the use of two breathing machines. The first was a ventilator, for use at night-time, to help Gwen's night-time breathing and to exercise/expand the lungs. The aim was to use it for six hours, but Gwen never managed more than two. She was also given a cough machine, to be used twice a day; this would measure her peak flow as she tried to cough into a mouthpiece while watching a movement on the screen of the machine.

12. Appointments

MY DIARY RECORDS a succession of appointments over the next few weeks.

October 15th 2019: a visit to a dietician in Zetland Street, Southport – just two minutes by car from home! The lady dietician was accompanied by a student from the University of Chester, who asked Gwen all the questions, with her mentor listening. They weighed Gwen at 7 stone (her best 'fighting weight' was about 9 and a half stone or 60 kilos!) and said they would prescribe supplement drinks to add to her list of medication.

October 21st and an appointment for 3.30 p.m. with Dr Finegan at the Hospice. However, at 3.35 she emerged into the waiting lounge and went to another family who had also been waiting. A nurse came to explain that after that family there was somebody else scheduled to see the doctor before us, so it would probably be at least another hour before we could see her. It was agreed that another appointment should be made.

Dr Finegan very kindly rang us at 6.15 to apologise for being so far behind schedule. We realised that her appointments could never be programmed exactly, told her that there was no need to apologise and we appreciated her call.

October 28th 2019. Another 'quick' trip to Aintree to pick up an oximeter to monitor the oxygen level in Gwen's blood overnight. And then another 'quick' trip to return the machine before 11 a.m. the next say.

The appointment with Dr Finegan was rescheduled for November 4th. We updated her on the two days in the VIC and the use of the two breathing machines. The occupational therapist was available while we were at the hospice and she gave Gwen a variant of a drinking cup to try. The apparently simple process of putting a cup to one's lips and sipping from it had become almost impossible for Gwen, as the muscles in mouth, lips, tongue and throat were all deteriorating. And this cup wasn't the answer. Opening tins had become a problem, and the therapist recommended an electric tin opener. We bought one on the way home.

November 6th 2019. Yet another department of Aintree hospital: the Elective Care Centre, round the back of the main building. With our recently acquired Blue Badge, we were able to park in a 'Disabled' space in front of the building next to Elective Care.

Our appointment was with nutrition consultant Dr Gledhill and her dietician. Gwen's struggles with normal eating required either a PEG or a RIG. I can't remember what the letters stand for, but apparently a PEG has a tube going in the mouth and down the throat to the stomach, whereas a RIG is a tube fitted directly into the stomach. Gwen would need the latter because of problems in the mouth/throat area. She would go into the VIC again for 48 hours; the tube would be fitted under local anaesthetic and it might be painful for the first 24-48 hours. If she could still manage to eat normally, she should keep doing so. The RIG would supplement her diet to make up for any deficiencies.

With hindsight, I wonder whether Gwen had quietly decided that the best way to end the torture of MND was to eat less and less, because taking in food had become such a frustratingly slow and messy job anyway. She would be able to decide how much to have inserted through the stomach tube, thereby not having to prolong the agony.

> *But food does not bring us near to God; we are no worse if we do not eat, and no better if we do. [1 Corinthians 8:8]*

The context here is whether or not to eat food sacrificed to idols! I accept that I have wrenched the words out of context, but there is an underlying truth here also about the centrality of the material world in people's thinking. Jesus was very clear in Matthew 6: 25-27: 'Therefore, I tell you, do not worry about your life, what you will eat or drink, or about your body, what you will wear. Is not life more important than food, and the body more important than clothes?' He then uses birds as examples of non-worriers that don't have a problem finding food and says that we are much more valuable in God's eyes than birds. He goes on to spell out the true priority: 'But seek first his [God's] kingdom and his righteousness, and all these things will be given to you as well. Therefore do not worry about tomorrow, for tomorrow will worry about itself. Each day has enough trouble of its own.' [Matthew 6: 33-34]

13. Therapies

NOVEMBER 13TH 2019 saw us at the hospice for an appointment with Jane Boulton, the complementary therapist. The title intrigued me, but it simply covered a range of options that might perhaps come under the heading of 'fringe medicine'. Reflexology didn't sound too 'new age', so that was Gwen's first choice: a massage of the feet with orange and lavender oils. Jane had a pleasant, easy manner and we both felt we could enjoy conversation with her.

I recalled representing our church at a 'Mind, Body and Spirit' event in the Floral Hall in Southport some years earlier. I was working in our Healing Rooms team at the time and prepared a paper on the value of healing as part of Christian ministry. When I found the room where I would present my paper, there were perhaps 6 or 8 people there, but as soon as I told them I was from the Community Church, a Christian who believed in healing in the name of Jesus Christ, most of the audience departed. I had the chance to look around the stalls of other groups and was interested to see that the ones with the longest queues were the ones that charged money for their particular therapy. Our ministry was free, but nobody wanted it! Reiki, yoga, acupuncture and other things were becoming very popular, but presumably people assumed that the Christians didn't have anything worthwhile to offer.

> *Heal the sick, raise the dead, cleanse those who have leprosy, drive out demons. Freely you have received, freely give. [Matthew 10:8]*

For her second session with Jane Boulton, Gwen opted for a neck and shoulder massage, which Jane said should be helpful for her breathing. And so it proved. Gentle background music created a pleasant atmosphere, and Gwen had some say in the variety of aromas to be included in the massage oil. I had tears in my eyes when I saw how skeletal her back and shoulders had become. But certainly, Gwen noticed that after a massage she could go several hours without needing to use her inhaler.

I had wondered how the hospice could afford to offer all these services free of charge, but I later discovered that you could have up to five sessions without payment, but after that you would have to pay. Hospices receive about 25-30% of their income from the government, with the rest coming from donations. I don't know how many staff Queenscourt has in total, but we must have encountered about a dozen by the time Gwen's ultimate stay came to an end. And then of course they have volunteers assisting in various ways. From now on, my first port of call when looking to take some stock to a charity shop would be the three Queenscourt shops around Southport.

As well as further beneficial massages from Jane Boulton, Gwen had a couple more Aintree trips to talk to doctors or nurses about the two breathing machines. The one she was supposed to wear through the night was of no value: she was meant to keep it on for up to six hours, but the feel of the thing on her head and the slight hum that the machine made prevented her from sleeping much, if at all. So Dr Plant, in the Sleep Laboratory, told her to stop trying to use it. The cough machine, however, was worth persevering with, because it was preventative rather than curative. If saliva keeps trickling down into the lungs it can create a pool, which can become infected and lead to pneumonia. The cough machine – three cycles twice a day – would help to avoid that possibility, although it wasn't easy for Gwen to produce a meaningful cough. She was told she would need the breathing machine when she had the RIG fitted, as a support for her lungs.

14. The feeding tube

DECEMBER 9TH 2019. We were now able to use a blue badge which allowed us to park in 'Disabled' spaces, and so we were blessed to find a space within a few metres of the main entrance to Aintree Hospital for Gwen's admission for the RIG to be fitted. It would have been a nightmare to carry the breathing machine, the cough machine and Gwen's case over any distance, but she was able to wheel the case while I carried the machines. She was again in the Ventilation Inpatient Centre on the first floor, close to the main entrance; she felt more comfortable knowing some of the nurses from her previous stay.

A student nurse from Edge Hill University took Gwen through a lengthy questionnaire; then there was a chest x-ray, the taking of a blood sample and her weight. She became quite emotional at times. She was initially on the open ward, so as to be under more immediate scrutiny. She managed to mash some potato into the soup which they brought her, but getting it down her throat was a major undertaking and not exactly a success. Before I left her, a nurse had kindly got her on to wifi with her iPad and phone. The procedure the next day would involve inserting a tube up the nose and down the throat into the stomach, so as to inflate the stomach for the RIG to be fitted more easily. She would have a local anaesthetic, with the breathing machine on hand.

December 10th. The procedure took place at 12.30. She said afterwards it was like being in a busy railway station, as there were so many people buzzing about, all talking – quite a noisy operation! Afterwards she was moved into a side room, similar to the one she had had previously. Despite a noisy air conditioning machine, she probably slept better in that room than in the open ward.

December 11th. I arrived at Aintree about 11.45 and found – again - a space within 40 metres of the front door, praise God.

The long ward of the VIC had visitors – a BBC film crew recording for the BBC2 programme 'Hospital', although not in the area where Gwen's room was. Her soup and baked potato arrived soon after me. We both had to learn how to use the RIG, so we had one trial run before lunch. I was happy to make use of the little Starbucks café on the ground floor, more or less under the VIC. They had put Gwen on paracetamol to ease the pain of the insertion.

We both passed the second trial run using the feeding tube into her stomach, so we were able to leave about 3.40 p.m.. Special bottles of Ensure in various flavours were provided to be put through the RIG by means of a syringe. They were to supplement whatever Gwen could manage to eat by normal means. Syringes would be posted to us – one per day and then discard! The nurse cleaned the wound and applied a very extensive waterproof dressing all round it.

A week later, a dietician came. We had got into a routine with the tube and syringes, usually about 10 a.m. and 8 p.m.. The dietician said there was no need for distilled water, that boiled tap water was fine for the initial and final flush of the syringe; also, a syringe could be used for up to a week! Certainly more economical than the hospital had said.

We also had the first of many visits from a district nurse, to check the wound and replace the dressing.

December 19th saw us back at the hospice with Dr Finegan. The questions this time were focused on Gwen's mental state, so there were moments of tears. Gwen had to fill in a questionnaire designed to measure levels of depression and anxiety. Both came up as 'mild' or 'very mild', so it was not deemed necessary to prescribe antidepressants.

> *You will keep in perfect peace the one whose mind is steadfast, because (s)he trusts in you. [Isaiah 26:3]*

Gwen was able to enjoy another neck and back massage, this time with a different lady who had a slightly different technique.

More than one person commented during these months of MND how resilient Gwen was, and she certainly never complained or asked 'Why me?' As her physical faculties declined, she maintained her mental sharpness and quietly got on with doing the things she could still manage to do. From this point on, however, our home was increasingly being 'invaded' by district nurses, palliative nurses, Abbott nurses (changing the tube of the RIG) and then, eventually, carers also. With the feeding routines and all these appointments and visits, our time was no longer our own. So many people were so intent on helping Gwen to be as comfortable as possible when, on the inside, she was probably crying out, 'Thanks, but just leave me alone now to die in peace.'

My soul is in anguish. How long, O Lord, How long?
[Psalm 6:3]

15. District nurses

JANUARY 2020. INITIALLY we had weekly visits by district nurses to check the RIG. The inner end of the tube – inside the stomach – is a little balloon, and the nurses' syringe should extract five millilitres of fluid and insert another five. If the extracted amount goes too low, the tube needs to be replaced. The tube would automatically be replaced after about ten weeks. The first time for Gwen's tube to be replaced, she would need to go to Aintree – only a brief visit – and thereafter, nurses could do it.

January 8th 2020. Dr Gledhill, at the Elective Care Unit at Aintree, was happy with the tube. Gwen's weight 'stable' at 44 kilos, or 6 stone 13 pounds.

February 6th 2020. Dr Finegan at the Hospice checked different things, including Gwen's bowels, which had always been unpredictable, pre-MND, and were increasingly a concern. Gwen had little or no padding in her buttocks, and sitting for any length of time made the coccyx – some call it the tail-bone - sore and the skin become red. She tried various creams and two kinds of padded cushion to sit on.

Dr Finegan also mentioned a group therapy day which they have at the hospice – a variety of activities that you can try, with no pressure; just whatever's best for each individual. Gwen seemed moderately interested initially, but when it came to the day, she decided not to go. I think she didn't particularly want to be surrounded by other MND patients or to have the inevitable well-meaning 'How ARE you?' approaches from nurses and/or volunteers.

February 19th 2020. Elective Care Centre at Aintree and Lisa, a nutritionist, was given the job of changing Gwen's RIG tube for the first time. She was very businesslike, putting Gwen at her ease by saying, 'It's just like having a stud replaced in your ear.' And it was – very straightforward, quick and painless. Deflating the inner balloon makes it easy to slip the tube out. Lisa said that the next time it needed replacing, an Abbott nurse would come to the house to do it. She thought district nurses were mostly a bit wary about doing the procedure, although when we mentioned it, our district nurses all seemed quite happy to do it.

March 5th. Angela McKenna, senior palliative nurse at Queenscourt, came for a catch-up. She too mentioned the group therapy activities, which Gwen could try out even for an hour.

March 12th. To the Sid Watkins Centre at Aintree for an appointment with Professor Young. She told us we probably wouldn't see her again as she was going to concentrate more on research. Her main concern was Gwen's weight loss: now down to 41.9 kilos. She suggested that we ask the dietician to call and see about having more of the Ensure bottles, perhaps three times a day instead of two.

Gwen's dry mouth, combined with the constant production of saliva, was an ongoing nuisance. The professor surprised us by saying that water was not the best thing for Gwen to drink. As it goes into the mouth and throat it breaks into droplets, which can go down the wrong way. Coughing and gasping for breath can be very frightening, she said, and we had already had some experience of exactly that. I had more than once had to smack/stroke Gwen's back between the shoulders to help her to breathe after a coughing bout. Definitely scary.

> *When he passes me, I cannot see him; when he goes by, I cannot perceive him. If he snatches away, who can stop him? Who can say to him, "What are you doing?" [Job 9: 11-12]*

April 6th. The dietician recommended three tube feeds per day. Also, as the district nurse had extracted just 4 millilitres from the balloon, the dietician contacted the Abbott nurse to come and change the tube.

16. No Covid, just MND

THE NATION WAS now in a coronavirus lockdown, so all nurses came wearing masks and PPE, taking every precaution to sanitise and to keep a distance. [Our sons and their families all caught Covid – more than once – but Gwen and I were spared that further complication.]

The Abbott nurse visited from Chester. She had rung beforehand to ask me to have a new RIG unpacked and at the ready (it had already come through the post to be available at any time). I had opened the wrapper, thinking I was helping, but the nurse said she would slap my leg if I opened a package again! She was laughing as she said it. She changed the tube very quickly and easily.

May 2020. In successive weeks, the district nurses extracted only just over four millilitres from the tube, but they didn't seem concerned.

June 4th 2020. Dr Finegan, on a video call, recommended ways of dealing with Gwen's bowel problems. Gwen said that showering and drying herself was becoming more difficult. (She always insisted that I should not get involved.) Dr Finegan said she would look into getting help for her.

June 8th. Rachel Barry came, recommended thickener in drinks yet again. Dietician Vicky rang and said Gwen should have one and a half Ensure bottles per feed, as one was not enough.

June 9th. The team leader of the district nurses called. If Gwen wanted help with showering, we would be means-tested, so we would have to pay. A phone call from Social Services later confirmed that to be the case. They gave me phone numbers for private care providers, but Gwen decided not to pursue that. She had hoped it would be within the remit of a district nurse, but apparently that would only apply if the patient was clearly within twelve weeks of dying!

June 25th 2020 (my 78th birthday). Amanda Grayshon, Queenscourt palliative nurse, on video call. We talked about Gwen's struggles with showering. She said she would call an occupational therapist to see if help could be provided.

June 26th. Gwen was convinced that fruit-flavoured Ensure drinks contributed to diarrhoea, so I rang the GP surgery to prescribe another lot, and then rang the pharmacy to ask them to limit flavours to vanilla, chocolate and neutral.

July 2nd. Dr Finegan on video call: drinks, dribbling, difficulty in shower. Gwen's loss of grip meant she was finding it hard to depress the end 'button' on her inhaler, so I was starting to do that for her. Dr Finegan suggested a nebuliser could be provided, but Gwen didn't want that at this stage.

July 6th. Imogen Baddeley, physiotherapist at Queenscourt, came to assess Gwen's needs. This young lady was always bright, positive, with a 'can-do' mentality. So, for drying herself after a shower, Gwen could be wrapped in a towelling bathrobe. And a seat in the bath would make showering more comfortable. As for the inhaler, and the need to use it twice every four hours, Imogen also recommended a nebuliser; she would talk to Dr Finegan about it.

July 10th. Imogen rang, having agreed with Dr Finegan that Gwen would benefit from a nebuliser. It had to be prescribed by a GP, so I rang the surgery, and they said Dr Tobin would ring me on the 14th.

That meant for the next four nights I would have to be available during the night to depress the inhaler twice for Gwen. As it happened, I woke to use the bathroom at around 3 a.m. each night, which was the optimum time! (Gwen had a little bell, which I said she should use if I stayed asleep; she wasn't keen to use it, so I'm glad she didn't need to.)

July 15th. Nebuliser delivered. Next we needed the solution to go in it.

Coming Through the Valley

July 16th. I rang the surgery to ask for a prescription for the nebuliser solution; the receptionist said she would mark it as 'Urgent'. I called at the pharmacy later that day and it was there.

July 17th. Assembling the nebuliser looked a bit complicated for my little brain, so I rang the district nurses' number and one of them came in the afternoon to set it up and show me how it worked.

August 19th. Gwen was struggling with a rattly cough and had not slept well; she couldn't get rid of anything. We were wondering who best to contact when I saw on the calendar that the palliative nurse was due that very day. And before lunchtime, Amanda Grayshon duly came. God's timing is always spot on.

She had various suggestions: patches on the side of the neck can reduce saliva; maybe another nebula to alternate; pull-ups (to guard against bowel accidents); a mild sleeping potion that could be taken via the RIG.

Amanda also mentioned that Queenscourt offered relaxation sessions via Zoom, and Gwen thought she would like to try that.

The hospice also offered a sit-in service, so that a carer – that's me - could have a couple of hours of respite from patient responsibility. I was grateful for the offer, but said that I did get out for a 20-minute bike ride or to go shopping, as well as some church meetings.

September 3rd. Video appointment with Dr Finegan. Re bowels: she would see if there was a mild form of Imodium that could be taken through the tube. (There was: I collected from pharmacy 2 days later.)

Gwen's experience working at Chase Heys Respite Centre came in very useful at this point. She asked Dr Finegan whether she qualified for Community Health Care – something I knew nothing about. The doctor said that she would indeed qualify and said she would set things in motion. It turned out that a terminally ill patient who might otherwise be cared for in hospital could instead be cared for at home on the same basis; i.e. free of charge.

Two days later, September 5th, we had a visit from the leader of the district nurses' team, Clare Smith, to assess Gwen's needs. She was happy to arrange for carers to come to the house each morning for getting Gwen up, washing or showering and dressing; another evening visit to put her to bed. Clare also said she would order a special mattress to try and alleviate the redness and soreness of Gwen's bottom; she didn't want the skin to break. A special cream could also help (another nurse delivered this the next day - Sunday morning).

17. Carers in the house

SEPTEMBER 8TH **2020**. The first two carers arrived when Gwen, who had become tired of waiting, was half-dressed, so there wasn't much for them to do, but at least they met her and knew where the house was. Two different carers came at 8.45 p.m. to get her undressed.

The special mattress had arrived today, and the kind delivery man without hesitation offered to help me take it upstairs and put it in position.

September 10th. Amanda Grayshon, palliative nurse, called. Gwen mentioned her sore bottom in the coccyx area. Amanda said she would order an air cushion to relieve the pressure. To help Gwen's dry mouth she suggested pineapple chunks in their own juice – not syrup: just have them in the mouth to suck and then spit out. I bought some and Gwen quite enjoyed the taste and feel of them.

Sadly, by September 25th, she had stopped using the pineapple chunks as they gave her a sore mouth.

We had now had carers twice a day for about three weeks. Arrival times varied, which was to be expected. We only said anything when they arrived about 7.30 p.m. to get her ready for bed! Yesterday we had to have the Abbott nurse come to replace the RIG, as it was completely blocked during a feed and had had only a 3.5 ml extraction by the district nurse.

Gwen now had a more effective cushion, courtesy of Imogen, and special cream for her bottom. She was also able to join in with a Queenscourt relaxation session via Zoom. I found it quite funny. After a minute or two of Hellos and getting in a comfortable position, the nurse read a narrative describing a walk into a country area, with all the things one could see and hear, etc.. She read it as if the listeners were two-year-olds – which is why I had to leave the room to stop laughing out loud. Anyway, Gwen appreciated it and felt relaxed.

September 26th. Imogen and a lady colleague came to fit the bath board, but our bath was slightly too wide, so the board wouldn't fit properly. Imogen suggested a swivel chair might be the answer: Gwen was delighted.

Imogen also recommended a 'profile bed'; i.e. a hospital bed, with a removable side rail and adjustable positions. The question was: should it be put in the bedroom or downstairs? Gwen didn't want to be in bed downstairs yet, although she knew it might become necessary at some stage. I needed to get one of the twin beds out of the front bedroom, then let Imogen know and she would have the profile bed delivered and set up.

District nurse Bernadette was back from holidays and called to check on Gwen. She said there was an inhaler that didn't need finger pressure, just a breath in and out would operate it. It later transpired, however, that Dr Finegan didn't think Gwen would have a strong enough puff to operate it.

We obviously didn't realise at the time, but Gwen was almost into her final two months of coping with MND. We were constantly remarking how so many people were doing their level best to make the ride as comfortable as possible, for me as well as Gwen.

> *Blessed are the people whose God is the Lord.*
> *[Psalm 144:15]*

18. Steady deterioration

SEPTEMBER 30TH 2020. Two men delivered the profile bed – lots of parts to carry up and then assemble in the bedroom, with a lead to an electrical socket. I was glad it didn't depend on me: far too complicated.

October 1st. Imogen and a colleague came to show us how to operate the moving parts of the bed. The motor had a very quiet hum, but not enough to disturb Gwen's sleep. For a day or two, Gwen felt the bed was lumpy and quite firm, but the air pump adjusts to the contours of the body, so it became more comfortable.

The ladies also fitted the swivel chair on the bath and showed us how to operate it. They had also borrowed from Queenscourt a sturdy plastic step for getting out of the bath more easily.

October 2nd. With the help of a carer, Gwen had a first shower using the swivel chair.

October 16th. When Bernadette called, Gwen expressed concern about shortness of breath and lack of energy. Her oxygen level was checked: 97% - very good. Bernadette said she would contact Dr Tobin to see about a blood test to see if she lacked iron.

October 18th. (Sunday) At Gwen's request, I rang the district nurses' number, as Bernadette had said she would be on duty. She duly came in the afternoon, dressing Gwen's coccyx; Gwen thought the air cushion had deflated. She encouraged Gwen to use the nebuliser more often, as it would break up the congestion and free the airways better than an inhaler.

October 22nd. Amanda had recommended glycerine mouth swabs to ease Gwen's dryness and control dribbling. I tried two local chemists without success. Eventually, Boot's pharmacy in the town centre found some, although not until the assistant had gone into an upstairs storeroom to hunt for them.

October 28th. On this day, I had been out at the church centre doing some teaching with three interns who were spending a year with us. On returning home, I found Gwen struggling to breathe or to cough, with saliva in her throat. I prayed for immediate relief – and there was some – but we agreed that we should seek further help. Gwen suggested district nurses, but I wasn't convinced they would be able to do the necessary, so I rang 111 [the emergency helpline for the NHS]. A man asked a lot of questions, then eventually he said he would send an ambulance.

A paramedic arrived about an hour later. He was excellent: calm, reassuring, businesslike. After he had checked Gwen, he rang Norwood surgery, as it was now 6.15 p.m. and he knew the surgery closed at 6.30. He knew the doctor, Dr Byrne, to whom he spoke. He said he had heard something on Gwen's lungs and asked Dr Byrne to prescribe antibiotics. He could have left me to carry on from that point, but insisted he would pick up the prescription and drive to Tesco pharmacy to get the antibiotics. On his return, he said we were entirely correct to have an ambulance sent out via 111. This method was much better than both of us going to Accident & Emergency at night, waiting probably several hours, mixing with other patients, and susceptible to catching Covid or something else. Meanwhile, if Gwen continued to struggle for breath, I should ring 999 and an ambulance would take her in to hospital.

As he left, he said that Dr Byrne would ring us at 9.20 the next morning to check on Gwen and decide if a home visit was needed. I regret not noting this paramedic's name: he was compassionate, caring and went well beyond the call of duty.

October 29th. Dr Byrne rang. We agreed to wait and see how Gwen reacted to the antibiotics. Gwen stayed in pyjamas and dressing gown; she did come downstairs, but hardly moved all day.

On November 3rd we were into the last complete month that Gwen would have on this earth. Another struggle for breath late in the evening. I was in bed reading when I was aware of strange noises coming from the other bedroom. Gwen was sitting on the spare bed, absolutely desperate to get some air into her lungs. Despite my patting and stroking her back, she wasn't getting any relief, so I rang 999. The receptionist asked quick questions and then assured me an ambulance was on its way. She kept me talking, giving her updates until the paramedics arrived in under ten minutes. Gwen's condition had eased a little by then. They did their necessary checks – heart, blood pressure, oxygen levels in the blood, all OK.

Typically of Gwen, not wanting to be a burden to anyone, she wrote 'sorry' on her notepad; her powers of speech had disappeared long before then. The paramedics insisted we had done exactly the right thing, and if she had another attack, even within the hour, we should ring 999 again. They said they would sit in their ambulance to write up their notes before returning to us, so I took a book downstairs while they did so. Back to bed about 12.30 a.m.

November 5th. Video call with Amanda Grayshon, palliative nurse. She said that if Gwen had another attack, we should call the district nurses, who could use the emergency medication to calm things down. I had completely forgotten this: various packets of medication in reserve in a bag, which we had never used or even thought to use. Amanda would let Dr Finegan know about the two paramedic call-outs.

November 7th. Gwen was struggling with a rattly chest and inability to cough anything out. At 6 p.m. I rang the district nurses and two of them came at 7 p.m. The rattle had subsided by then. The nurses checked the reserve medication and found that one lot was out of date, so they arranged a replacement.

At bedtime, it was noticeable how slowly Gwen climbed the stairs; I stayed close behind her in case she lost her balance.

She had been out in the garden during the afternoon – without a coat – giving me instructions about what to do with various plants in pots over the winter months. Gwen was good with flowers; I struggled even to remember the names of some of them.

That morning, Gwen had enjoyed a shower, because her favourite carer, Bev, was on duty. Bev was one of the youngest of the carers that came to the house. We were amazed to learn that she had five children, aged between one and thirteen; that her previous partner had died and that her current partner was very understanding of the hours she worked. She had done 70 hours this week!

November 9th. Dr Finegan for an update on video call. Gwen mentioned the possibility of being admitted to the hospice. Did she have an inkling that the end was not far away? The doctor said there were pros and cons, one of the latter being that there were no visitors during this Covid lockdown. She suggested having Gwen's bed downstairs, but Gwen didn't want that just yet. The doctor also said that it would be OK –Covid-wise - for one of our sons to visit and sit with Gwen if I had to go out; or the hospice could have somebody call to sit with her. So much help! So kind! And if there was another emergency, we could call 999 or district nurses or Queenscourt to get help.

November 20th. Helen, one of the district nurses, visited. Mention was made of the hospice and the palliative nurses. She said she would speak to Amanda about Gwen. Later, Amanda rang to say that Gwen could be admitted the next day for two weeks' monitoring and respite care; she emphasised that the respite was for both of us! Gwen said Yes without hesitation.

19. Into the hospice

NOVEMBER 21ST 2020. When I took Gwen in to Queenscourt Hospice for 10 a.m. I had no idea that she was leaving our home for the last time. And when I parked close to the entrance, she then took the final steps that she would walk on this earth. I was not able – because of Covid lockdown restrictions – to go in with her.

Only one person at a time could visit, by phoning to agree a time. I went at 2.30, not allowed inside; I had to wear full PPE – a plastic full-length apron, a face mask and gloves, all disposable. I had a temperature check and had to walk round the outside of the building and then sit on a plastic chair outside the closed patio door at the end of the ward. Communication was laboured. Gwen had to write everything down and hold it up towards the patio door. A nurse had opened a small top window, so I could just make myself heard inside. Later, our younger son John and his family had a Facetime contact with Gwen; I could hear but not see them.

November 22nd. John visited with me, both sitting outside again. When we came away, he was a bit tearful: 'You're used to seeing her; I'm not,' he said.

Tim – our elder son - brought me some food and a lovely crocheted rug that Katie had made. He also had a tearful moment. Both boys loved their dear mum.

Gwen had slept through the night until 5 a.m. without any breathing aid. Her medication included some morphine to help her breathing be more relaxed, and it also helped her to sleep. The only downside was that she still felt rather sleepy during the day.

November 23rd. Imogen Baddeley, the hospice physiotherapist, had spoken to Gwen about having the profiling bed brought downstairs. And she had asked about me sleeping downstairs as well, to be available with the inhaler as and when required? Or maybe a district nurse could visit at, say, 3 a.m. to administer the inhaler? They really were doing everything they possibly could.

November 27th. It had been agreed that the bed should be taken downstairs, so two men came to dismantle, carry down and reassemble it in the dining room extension. They also brought an adjustable bed table and a wheelchair commode. Clearly, there was an expectation at this point that Gwen would return from Queenscourt. Imogen again was responsible for the extras; she was so good at thinking of ways to help beyond the obvious.

When I visited the hospice – again in full PPE with a temperature check, even though still required to stay outside the patio door – Gwen looked ill. I knew they had put her on oxygen the day before to help her breathing, but now she was too tired to communicate by writing, so we texted each other. One of the last things she had written on her pad was 'Donation Que 't [meaning Queenscourt] …' and a substantial amount she was suggesting. I was able to let her know that I had anonymously donated that exact amount two days earlier.

Dr Maarten Scholten was on duty and asked to speak to me. We were outside, but near enough for Gwen to realise what he was saying. He gently expressed his opinion that Gwen could well be on the last lap. He asked if I wanted them to keep on ventilating her lungs indefinitely, and I said No. I told him she had a strong Christian faith and was not afraid of death. I shed a few tears during the conversation, aware now that the long cruelty of MND was nearing its end.

> *The Lord is my light and my salvation – whom shall I fear? The Lord is the stronghold of my life – of whom shall I be afraid? [Psalm 27:1]*

Gwen texted me that she didn't want dramatic farewells and not to let the grandchildren come to the hospice. She wasn't even sure that Tim and John should visit again, as they were planning to do in the next couple of days. We blew kisses to each other before I left.

Many waters cannot quench love; rivers cannot wash it away. [Song of Songs 8:7]

November 28th. It was Saturday, and when I phoned Queenscourt there was only a recorded message, so I didn't visit. I later realised that I had been phoning the palliative nurses' number rather than Reception. My brother Paul rang me, so I told him what the doctor had said. Likewise I phoned Tim and John, and also spoke to Gwen's sister-in-law, Norma.

November 30th. Gwen seemed a bit brighter and we texted each other for a while until it rained. I was still confined to the patio because of Covid restrictions.

It seemed that the conversation with the doctor was an 'If' rather than a 'When', preparing the way in case Gwen deteriorated rapidly.

The social worker had been talking to Gwen, asking where she would like to go when she left the hospice. I suppose this was normal procedure, and they were not to know how much longer Gwen would be with us. Gwen's view – and I agreed with her – was that she now needed more care than visiting carers and I could supply, so we should look for a nursing home. Gwen had in mind a new home in Park Road, which she asked me to look up. When I got home, I did so: Parklands Lodge had 70 beds and they did take patients with motor neurone disease.

December 1st. Imogen phoned to ask me to take in the cough machine, which she would adjust to try and help Gwen.

We had a texting conversation at my 2 p.m. visit. I told her about a lovely email from David and Debora Lyon, church leaders down in the Midlands, and also a message from other dear friends, John and Julie Anderson. Julie had taught in the Junior department at Scarisbrick Hall School. She and John had lived with us for a short period when they needed accommodation, and they were members of the Community Church until they moved to the south of England.

I had alerted the church elders to the conversation I had had with the doctor, so they had asked the church to have three days of prayer and fasting on Gwen's behalf. No stone was left unturned.

December 2nd. Covid restrictions had changed today, so I was able to sit just inside the patio door for the first time, although not close to the bed. I was very grateful for that. Dr Scholten and Imogen both appeared. The doctor said there were no immediate plans for Gwen to be moved on from the hospice. They knew that she didn't have long to go now and they were confirming that in my thinking. Very gentle, rather subtle – they are so good at what they do.

One of the prayer aids I use is the CARE Prayer Diary, and this week they included this quote from Joni Eareckson Tada, a Christian lady who in her youth had dived into the sea, struck a rock and been quadraplegic for the rest of her life:-

> 'I, with shrivelled, bent fingers, atrophied muscles, gnarled knees, and no feeling from the shoulders down, will one day have a new body, light, bright and clothed in righteousness – powerful and dazzling. Can you imagine the hope this gives? No other religion … promises new bodies, hearts and minds. Only in the Gospel of Christ do hurting people find such incredible hope.'

How timely was that?!

December 4th. When I visited, Gwen was lying on her side, with mouth wide open, unresponsive since our final exchange of love messages by text.

20. The agony ends

SATURDAY 5TH DECEMBER 2020. I was now able to visit as long as I wanted, via the patio door, and sitting just inside. This time, however, they had moved the bed closer to the door, so the nurse encouraged me to hold Gwen's hand. I read some Bible verses to her. Her eyes were partly open, but not seeing anything earthly; I like to think she was already seeing the welcoming arms of her Saviour. Her mouth was open as well, silently singing praises to God.

> *After this I looked, and there before me was a door standing open in heaven. (Revelation 4:1]*

The nurses left me alone with Gwen, so I was noticing details in the room. On the side rail of the bed was a little sticker notice which said it was 'a potential entrapment hazard', but I was feeling relieved that at last Gwen was being set free from the entrapment hazard of motor neurone disease. And there was no hazard in her onward journey through the curtain of death.

> *Even though I walk through the valley of the shadow of death, I will fear no evil, for you are with me; your rod and your staff, they comfort me. [Psalm 23:4]*

I registered the fact that she had fought a good fight, in true Salvationist style; she was finishing her race here and winning a great victory.

A wonderful wife

A marvellous mother

A glorious grandma

The nurses had beautifully chosen Classic FM as the station playing quietly above Gwen's head. I turned it up slightly; Beethoven's 'Moonlight Sonata' came on, a piece that both of us loved.

Dr Scholten appeared and immediately spoke to Gwen. He encouraged me to do the same, as she would very probably be able to hear and understand anything that was said. We talked about music and singing, about grandchildren and gardening.

About mid-day I went home for a break. At about 1.30 I had a text from John asking if he could visit Mum. Although Gwen had not wanted the boys to see her in the final stages, I felt it was right if they were keen to visit. I contacted Tim and we agreed to go at 2.30. When I rang Queenscourt, the nurse didn't like the idea of three visitors, although I said we would go in relays. When I said 2.30, she at first said No, because the lady in a bed nearby was having a visitor at 2.15. She suggested 3.30, but sensed my hesitation, spoke to a colleague and then agreed to 2.30.

There were now two chairs inside the patio doors, close to the bed, so Tim and John, with full PPE regalia, had time with Gwen together. I had told them how she would look and encouraged them to talk to her.

After they left, both having shed tears, I sat with her. It was very peaceful. I could see a pulse in her neck which still seemed strong, but her breathing through her open mouth was very shallow. Eventually her jaw twitched a couple of times and her breathing stopped. I pressed the button for the nurse, who came quickly. I said I thought Gwen had gone, and she confirmed it. Gone to a far better place. Gone to the glorious Presence of the King of kings Himself!

> *I have fought the good fight, I have finished the race, I have kept the faith. Now there is in store for me the crown of righteousness, which the Lord, the righteous Judge, will award to me on that day – and not only to me but also to all who have longed for his appearing. [2 Timothy 4:7-8]*

The nurse asked me to leave the ward for about fifteen minutes while they carried out the necessary checks and did the paperwork. I went to the car and made several calls on my mobile phone.

The word 'serenity' comes to mind as I reflect on those minutes. Nineteen years previously, when Gwen and I had been on holiday in Israel – we were actually by the Sea of Galilee at the time - I had to take a phone call from Dave Gregg in the UK to tell me that Linda Bisset, from our church, had died suddenly in the night, leaving a husband and four children. They wanted me to know as the family had asked for me to take the funeral. When I walked back to tell, firstly, Gwen, and then our good friends John and Julia, who were also in the tour party, it took me quite a while to get a grip of my emotions and blurt out the news of Linda's death.

But now, as I spoke to Tim, to John, to David Harlow, Gwen's brother, to Geoff Grice, our church leader, to my brother Paul and to my niece Helen, I was calmness personified. Amazing! Many people's prayers were being answered in ways they might not have expected, had they known.

When I returned to the ward, the senior nurse said they would gather all Gwen's belongings and log them, so that I could collect them the following day. When she asked if we had a funeral director in mind, I said Howard's, and she gave me their phone number.

Yes, tears were shed at times during those hours, but Gwen's wish was fulfilled that there were no agonised bouts of loud sobbing

I was so grateful that John had requested a visit, and that he and Tim had been with their Mum just an hour before she left us. If the nurse had insisted on a 3.30 visit, it would have been too late.

When she was admitted to Queenscourt Hospice, the palliative nurse had said it was for two weeks' respite, for Gwen and for me. How wonderful that she left us on the final afternoon of those two weeks!

In the final 24 hours, the texts between us had been brief but precious – some of Gwen's were rather incoherent, either because the light was fading or because she could not control her fingers well enough.

My final message to her phone was: Ich lieber dich. Gwen had been fascinated by this phrase many years before – she thought the German was more expressive than the English 'I love you', so we used it in many special intimate moments. I'm so grateful that was the last message she would have seen on her mobile phone.

21. Good things to remember

AT SOME POINT in the next 24 hours, I sensed God telling me to write down as many good things as I could think of that came particularly out of Gwen's Queenscourt experience. She had queried how Romans 8:28 ('We know that all things work together for good for those who love God and are called according to his purpose') could really apply to her situation: how could anything good come out of a death by motor neurone disease? This is what I wrote down:-

1. She had always wanted to pass away in the hospice, and her wish was granted.

2. She had been able to go into Queenscourt on foot, not by ambulance or in a wheelchair.

3. She had had her full two weeks of hospice care.

4. She did not need to be transferred from the hospice to a care home, with all the attendant upheaval and adapting.

5. She had her wish not to be 'a burden to David' in those final two weeks. I had no feeding tube duties

or inhalers to press or nebulisers to switch on or district nurses to call.

6. She had Tim and John with her an hour before she left us.

7. She had me with her for her departure to better things.

8. She had never vomited. She hated vomiting.

9. She had no pain apart from the sore coccyx.

10. She had never needed me to help her on the toilet, something she regarded as the ultimate humiliation.

11. She was still able to send and receive texts the day before she left us.

12. The last message on her phone was my 'Ich lieber dich'.

13. She had asked, and was able to see both Dr Finegan and Imogen Baddeley in the hospice, as she really valued the help they had given us.

14. She was spared Covid 19, which took so many lives and wrecked so many families.

15. The grandchildren were spared the trauma of visiting her in the hospice.

16. She successfully completed her baby-sitting and school picking-up duties for all six of her grandchildren.

17. She was loved, prayed for and appreciated by so many, as the pile of cards, messages and letters testify.

With hindsight, I could well have added more. For example, the National Health Service, for all its faults, is still 'free at the point of delivery'. If we had lived in some other countries, how much would it have cost to have appointments with consultants, overnight stays in hospital, the use of a breathing machine and a nebuliser? Two weeks of hospice care, twenty-four hours each day, would have added to the cost, as would the provision of a hospital bed and various other pieces of equipment in our home. Visits from district nurses over several months, and from carers over several weeks, would not have come cheaply. I know I didn't enjoy paying for petrol and parking fees to deliver an oximeter to Aintree hospital, but really I am ashamed even to have had those thoughts. Not only was Gwen's care and treatment 100% free, but in fact we received carer's allowance of over £80 per week from the government – which means from taxpayers. I am truly grateful.

Some might see all that free provision as a kind of payback for our years of tithing. Gwen and I learnt to practise tithing when our boys were young, money was tight and the country had high inflation. The church of which I have been a member since its inception in 1983 has always encouraged and taught tithing. In Malachi chapter 3, 'the Lord Almighty' is recorded as rebuking his people because 'you have cheated me of the tithes and offerings due to me.' Some Christians dismiss tithing either because it is 'part of the law of Moses' which no longer applies in the new covenant, or because 'Jesus doesn't teach tithing'.

Both objections are inaccurate. Tithing predates Moses by several generations, going back to Abraham's freewill donation to Melchizedek [Genesis 14:20]. Certainly it was incorporated into the Mosaic law, but its origins are anything but legalistic. As for the teaching of Jesus on tithing, Matthew 23:23 could not be clearer. He is rebuking the Pharisees for their unbalanced priorities when he brands them as hypocrites. 'You are careful to tithe even the tiniest part of your income [other versions specify 'mint, dill and cumin'], but you ignore the important things of the law – justice, mercy and faith. ***You should tithe, yes,*** but you should not leave undone the more important things.' [New Living Translation]

The rebuke recorded in Malachi is followed by the most wonderful promise accompanied by a challenge: '"Bring all the tithes into the storehouse so there will be enough food in my Temple. If you do," says the Lord Almighty, "I will open the windows of heaven for you. I will pour out a blessing so great you won't have enough room to take it in! Try it! Let me prove it to you!" '

My experience endorses those words. Sometimes an unexpected financial blessing comes in; but it can also be money staying with us that we might have expected to have to pay out. Either way, I am happy to respond positively to God's challenge and to the words of Jesus that tithing into my storehouse – the church from which I am spiritually fed – releases heavenly resources which might otherwise be held back.

22. A simple cremation

GWEN HAD BEEN very clear about funeral arrangements. 'Just get them to put my body in a bag and get rid of it.' She had read somewhere that something along those lines was now becoming more popular, as people wanted to keep the astronomical costs of funerals down. When the boys and I went to meet the funeral director, we ensured that simplicity prevailed: no limos, as we would all use our own cars. Covid restrictions kept our numbers to thirty, although on the day the crematorium people said it could only be twenty-five seated inside the chapel and five would have to stay in the lobby, with the doors left open.

The service combined the ministries of Geoff, our senior elder in the church, and John, now retired from eldership but a long-standing friend. He has pretty well set the standard for eulogies at so many funerals over many years, and he used most of the information I supplied him with, as well as adding some personal touches. Gwen and I had agreed that the music would be the John Rutter version of 'All things bright and beautiful' and the chorus 'And the glory of the Lord shall be revealed' from Handel's *Messiah*.

It was only some time after the cremation – maybe two weeks, as Christmas took our attention just after it – when I realised that the funeral director had not asked what we wanted to do with Gwen's ashes. Gwen certainly didn't want them scattered in a 'special' place, so perhaps it was in God's overruling that we didn't have to decide what happened to them. I know people want to associate a dead person with a particular place, but Gwen knew – and we agreed – that her real life was continuing beyond any grave and that she would eventually have a resurrection body, which would be far superior to the shrunken skeleton that we had cremated.

My niece Helen had used her floristry skills brilliantly in producing just one magnificent arrangement of flowers, with some of the greenery coming from our garden. I was able to fill several vases at home afterwards.

There was no weeping and wailing at the cremation; Gwen did not want great shows of emotion. Some tears, of course, but a lovely sense of family coming together, along with the presence of long-time church friends.

I was more tearful when reading the many cards and letters that had arrived.

> *'Fear not, for I have redeemed you; I have summoned you by name; you are mine. When you pass through the waters, I will be with you; and when you pass*

through the rivers, they will not sweep over you. When you walk through the fire, you will not be burned; the flames will not set you ablaze. For I am the Lord your God, the Holy One of Israel, your Saviour....' [Isaiah 43: 1-3]

The Facebook phenomenon was an interesting one. I rarely post on there, but when Gwen passed away I wanted everyone not just to register the fact but also to know of our assurance that she was now enjoying a fullness of life and freedom far beyond anything she had experienced in this life. I have perhaps 150 former pupils as Facebook friends, most of them not Christians, so I wanted to get a message across to them without being too 'preachy'. Here is what I wrote on Facebook on December 6th 2020:-

> 'My favourite lady has – to use the Salvation Army terminology she grew up with – been promoted to glory. She lived bravely through nearly two and a half years of motor neurone disease but now she's free, she's free from lousy MND!

She took Jesus as her life companion at an early age and so we are convinced that she will fully enjoy being in the presence of the King of kings in eternity.

> We were into our 48th year of marriage: she was a wonderful wife, a marvellous mother and a

glorious grandma to our six grandchildren. It was a privilege to have shared life with her.'

I included photos of us on our wedding day, and Gwen having fun up a mountain and paddling in the sea, as well as guiding our youngest grandchild in crossing the road.

One hundred and ninety-eight comments brought tears to my eyes.

23. Celebration at last

IN THE MONTHS that followed, the 5th day of each month registered with me, without needing to write down any reminders. Then, on her birthday, November 15th, I posted again on Facebook, saying she would have been 75 but that time was now irrelevant for her and she would now be identifying 100% with these words from Psalm 16:11:

> *You have made known to me the path of life; you will fill me with joy in your presence, with eternal pleasures at your right hand.*

As Covid limitations had prevented many people from attending the cremation, the family and I had it in mind to hold a 'Gwen Celebration' for wider family and friends whenever the lockdown eased. We set the date for September 11th 2021, and the venue was to be the Family Life Centre, the home of Southport Community Church. Gwen had left some suggestions as to what might be included in such an event, and I was happy to comply.

An 11.30 start on a Saturday morning would give time for people to travel from a distance, and we had guests from South Wales, Cornwall, London and North Yorkshire, some of whom came up the day before. Brenda Sterling, who had been a close friend of Gwen's from late teens onwards, came from London, where she and her husband David had served in the Salvation Army Training College, as well as doing similar work in Africa.

We stressed that the Celebration was not a church service: we did not have singing for the folk who gathered, some of whom would have been quite unfamiliar with hymns or worship songs. We did play CDs of songs that meant a lot to Gwen and concluded with a chorus from Handel's *Messiah*: 'And the glory of the Lord shall be revealed.' Brenda spoke, as did Gwen's brother, David, about her early years. We also had an opportunity for others to contribute, and Norma, Gwen's sister-in-law, and Kathryn, Gwen's niece, spoke fondly of her. Two of our granddaughters read poems.

Our daughter-in-law Debs had the lovely idea of putting a little packet of flower seeds on each chair, so that people could take them away and plant them in memory of Gwen. Months later, I was sent photos of flowers that people had planted in their gardens. Those pictures prompted both a smile and a few tears.

I wrote a narrative of Gwen's life and entrusted the presentation of that to two of our church friends. Dave Gregg had been a pupil of mine at Scarisbrick Hall School, had joined the church in his student days and was now in his twenty-fifth year as an elder of the church. Debbie Nolan was the manager of a counselling charity in Southport, but it was in her other role as a hairdresser that she had been a regular visitor to our home to trim Gwen's hair. In that capacity she had been the only person from church able to visit Gwen regularly during the final months of her life, and both Gwen and I appreciated her visits. It says much for her character that she was willing to give up a working Saturday to be a narrator for the Celebration.

Eighty invited guests were able to enjoy a buffet lunch after the Celebration, served by church friends. Helen, my niece, once more provided beautiful flowers to decorate each table and window ledge. My son John and my grandson Jonathan accompanied themselves on guitars as they sang some Beatles songs during lunch, and we had two tables of photographs and interesting memorabilia on display.

24. Grief and gratitude

IT WAS ENTIRELY right that there were times of laughter during the day, as we recalled special moments in Gwen's life and paid tribute to her often unsung achievements. Tears? Yes, of course, but again – as Gwen had insisted throughout – no weeping and wailing. Positive appreciation of a life well lived was combined with the assurance that she was now free from MND and enjoying the rich blessings of life beyond death. In that context, grieving would have been saying, in effect, 'See what I have lost.' And in the tearful moments before and since that day, I have soon been able to focus much more on 'See what she has gained.'

This is in no way a criticism of those bereaved people who do take months or years to grieve over the loss of a loved one. We are all different, and our perceptions of life and death are very individual. I have recently read a book called *Love, Interrupted* by Simon Thomas. Simon was well known as a television presenter, first on the children's flagship programme *Blue Peter* and then anchoring coverage of live football on Sky Sports. His wife Gemma contracted acute myeloid leukaemia quite out of the blue and, within three days, she died, leaving Simon and their eight-year-old son, Ethan.

The book is a heart-wrenching account of Simon's battles with depression, which had started some time before Gemma's death, and then with the reality of a future in which he would have to bring up his son on his own. He writes as a Christian, and is very honest about the anger and horror he experienced in trying to process the sudden departure of his lovely wife. Reading his book made me even more grateful for the forty-seven years of marriage I had been granted, and it certainly softened my heart towards those whose bereavement is so shattering.

A further thought on grieving: if grief is an expression of sadness at someone's departure, then I may have done most of my grieving in the months *before* Gwen left us, because her physical presence had changed so noticeably that I was seeing a different person. Maybe it was during that period that I grieved for the lady I had loved for so many years, who was so full of life and character. In the final months, even normality had become an effort for her, and she hated being dependent - either on me, or on nurses and carers. She was normally the dependable one to whom others turned, but now, for instance, she was more likely to be a spectator of grandchildren's games rather than a willing participant.

Some time later I was reminded of King David's attitude when the baby he and Bathsheba had conceived was desperately ill. David had behaved abominably in committing, firstly, adultery with Bathsheba and then also murder in having her husband Uriah fatally abandoned on the battle-field. God prompted Nathan the prophet to confront David about his wickedness and to bring God's judgement on the situation: the baby boy would die, but David would live on. The record in 2 Samuel 12 describes how David fasted, pleaded with God, spent whole nights lying on the ground, but without his desired outcome. The boy died.

The change in David at that point was dramatic and drew comments and questions from his courtiers. He got up, washed, changed his clothes, went to the temple to worship, and had something to eat when he came back. In reply to the surprised questioners, he said, 'While the child was still alive, I fasted and wept. I thought, "Who knows? The Lord may be gracious to me and let the child live." But now that he is dead, why should I fast? Can I bring him back again?' All very logical, but some might accuse him of an apparent lack of feeling.

In my own situation, even while Gwen lay helpless in the hospice, there was still a tiny glimmer of hope that God might intervene miraculously. Once that hope had been extinguished by her passing, I received such a strong sense of reassurance that drew the sting out of her departure. The reassurance encompassed my lovely wife, now set free from the vileness of MND, and my own situation, in which the relief and thankfulness for Gwen's release balanced out my sense of loss. God had received a loved one to himself and I sensed immediately that this amazing God was more than capable of looking after her in the eternal realm and myself in the earthly realm.

25. Making adjustments

I WANTED TO CARRY on as normally as possible, to adjust older routines and to adapt to new ones. The landscape had changed again: major change required the balancing effect of steady continuity to maintain an even keel through the choppy waters. I would need to learn new roles and new rules if I was going to come through on the positive side, but that in itself represented a new adventure in the life of faith.

It certainly helped that Christmas came just twenty days after Gwen's departure. I had had the focus of singing and recording music for the church's Covid-adapted online output with the worship team. The writing of Christmas cards enabled me to tell friends about Gwen. And there was time to reflect before family gatherings over the holiday season.

Almost a year after Gwen's promotion to glory, I had an unexpected conversation with a wise Christian friend. His wife was at the time having chemotherapy for a rare kind of leukaemia, and he had counselled many people facing the reality of serious disease. He apologised if his words seemed inappropriate and then surprised me by saying, 'In reality, God was never going to heal Gwen miraculously.

If that had happened, the whole world would have been beating a path to your door. The television crews would swamp the place and we would never have coped with all the hullabaloo.'

One part of my mind had to agree with him, yet at the same time I found myself saying, 'Lord, please equip your church – particularly this church – to be ready for the day when such an outstanding miracle takes place.' I dare to believe that it will happen.

> *Then the angel showed me the river of the water of life, as clear as crystal, flowing from the throne of God and of the Lamb down the middle of the great street of the city. On each side of the river stood the tree of life, bearing twelve crops of fruit, yielding its fruit every month. And the leaves of the tree are for the healing of the nations. [Revelation 22: 1-2]*

The first big change I noticed in life without Gwen was just how many hours there are in a day. No more tube feeds to administer; no more inhalers to press or nebulisers to switch on and off. No more nurse visits or carers calling. So still. So quiet. In some ways, so empty. No routines existed now: I was free to choose how I would occupy myself every hour of every single day.

I have always been comfortable with my own company. A quiet house is unthreatening. Some people are programmed to live with constant noise: talking, singing, hearing music, listening or half-listening to television or radio. I enjoy some conversation, particularly if it includes some laughter, but I cannot just talk for the sake of filling a silence. Visiting sick people with Gwen in my years as a church elder was always something of a chore for me: I knew I should do it, and I was to a degree happy to do it, but I never mastered the art of small talk. Gwen used to play down her ministry in this area. I call it ministry because it is every bit as important as preaching a sermon or leading a prayer gathering. Whereas I could readily do the latter, she was an expert in the former. Sitting at a hospital bedside I would just marvel at the things she thought of to advance a conversation.

When I stepped away from being an elder, it was no longer expected of me that I would visit the sick; but the change didn't affect Gwen, who would still happily go off visiting.

Gwen's departure meant that I could decide entirely for myself when I would get up, what I would eat, what I might watch on television and when I would go to bed. Getting up at 6.30 a.m. had become a well-established habit; in fact, I now sometimes rose nearer 6 o'clock. The first hour of the day would always be my time with God, reading the Bible, praying and listening. That didn't change.

My soul yearns for you in the night; in the morning my spirit longs for you. [Isaiah 26:9]

In the morning, O Lord, you hear my voice; in the morning I lay my requests before you and wait in expectation. [Psalm 5:3]

Beyond that, my time was at my disposal. Where Gwen's needs had been uppermost, now there was a void. And, for all the loving support of family and friends, many days I was entirely on my own if I didn't have cause to leave the house.

I kept her glasses, her watch and her wedding ring on the chest of drawers in our bedroom. I didn't look at them often, but just knowing they were there was sufficient to remind me of her and at times the tears would flow when I did look. Other tearful times came when I would hear something that I would want to share with her, and I would have to confront the reality of her departure.

With the help of one of my daughters-in-law, we filled several bin bags with Gwen's clothes and I gradually removed them to one of the Queenscourt charity shops. There was no immediate need to dispose of other 'stuff', of which there was plenty in drawers, wardrobes, cupboards and boxes. Whereas I had taken over our small third bedroom and transformed it into a study, with a desk, books and files aplenty, Gwen had used a variety of locations for her belongings. It was several months after she'd gone when I opened a drawer in our bedroom to find two large manila envelopes: one labelled 'Penwortham', the other 'Aughton'. (Tim lived in Penwortham, John in Aughton.) She had divided up her necklaces, brooches and pendants as evenly as possible between our sons' families to avoid any squabbles. I handed the envelopes to each daughter-in-law for them to allocate to the grandchildren.

26. One year on

THE FIRST ANNIVERSARY of her departure came on Sunday 5th December 2021. Maureen Stoddart, our friend who had been the first to realise that Gwen had MND, had told me the week before that she would be away that day but would be praying for me. She had lost her husband, Alan, to cancer, twenty years ago and I have always admired her dignity in dealing with the loss of her spouse. Two other people gave me cards: one was a lifelong family friend – Carol - who had lost her husband just a couple of weeks after Gwen had left us; the other was Debbie, Gwen's hairdresser and a good friend.

The day itself was full of activity, which was probably a good thing. I was at the church meeting in the morning and I had been invited, along with four other 'golden oldies', to the home of a comparatively new couple for Sunday lunch. Andy and Jane Gibbs run a bed and breakfast establishment not far from the town centre, and they produced a sumptuous roast dinner, during which we were entertained by their young daughter as much as by our own conversation. None of those present would have realised that it was the anniversary of Gwen's passing, although a few days later, one of the ladies had seen it mentioned on Facebook and was apologising to me for not realising at the time. I reassured her that she could not be expected to know and I thanked her for her contribution to a happy time over lunch.

I returned home just before 4 p.m. and had just closed my eyes in anticipation of a few minutes' napping when there was a gentle tap on the window, and there were my two sons with families. They had agreed among themselves just to descend on me, with all elements needed for tea so that I didn't have to do anything. Another happy time, with lots of laughter.

Then at 7 p.m. I had a meeting of church life group leaders until about 9 p.m., so I hardly had time to pause and reflect all day. I did put a post on Facebook:-

> 'The first anniversary of Gwen's departure brings an element of grief, yes, but mainly gratitude. I think I grieved for her most while I saw what motor neurone disease was doing to her body. And there have been some tears in the past year. But I live now with so much gratitude:
>
> - that I was privileged to share my life with her
> - that she was such a good influence on so many
> - that she has been released from the scourge of MND
> - that her faith in Jesus has ensured a glorious future.

Those tambourines in the heavenly chorus must sound fabulous by now!'

One young lady, whose mother had been a member of our church and died in the past year or so at a similar age to Gwen, commented that she wished she could feel more gratitude, but for her the loss felt too overwhelming. I cannot criticise her: I am just aware that we are all different.

> *Be joyful always; pray continually; give thanks in all circumstances, for this is God's will for you in Christ Jesus. [I Thessalonians 5:16-18]*

We can give thanks *in* all circumstances, which is not the same as *for*!

27. Looking forward

ONE LESSON I HAVE learned in dealing with Gwen's departure is that the pathway to recovery is also a journey of discovery. I can never return to life exactly as it was before Gwen was stricken with MND, but to what extent would I really want to? Life, as they say, moves on. Time passes. Seasons change. The cells in our bodies are perpetually dying and being replaced. I believe it would be wrong to want to cling to a particular stage in life's journey, because every stage is transitory, with or without the intervention of a terminal illness.

I have heard it said many times that constant change is here to stay, and I know that for some people adapting to change is very hard. I have given talks on that very topic to groups who are at or near 'retiring age', because it can be a difficult process.

Our response to change depends to some degree on whether the focus of our lives is mainly forward or backward. If nostalgia is the abiding undercurrent of your life, you may find it hard to face an uncertain future. For myself, although I have now reached 80 years of age, I am still looking forward each day. I mean that in the literal sense – so, when somebody says 'Have you had a good week?' I genuinely have to pause and make some effort to recall what the past week has brought.

But I am also 'looking forward' in the same way that a child looks forward to Christmas. It is in the core of my being that God has better and greater things in store than we have seen and experienced so far. 'The best is yet to be' may slip easily from the tongue, but for me it's far more than wishful thinking – it's a deep conviction. And if my starting-point is two years and four months observing my sweetheart having the life gradually squeezed out of her by MND, then it is not hard to believe that better things will follow.

There are some biblical texts which seem to be taken up by so many people – sometimes, perhaps, in desperation – as if to twist God's arm and demand a positive outcome to a difficult situation. One such verse is in Jeremiah 29:11: *'For I know the plans I have for you,' declares the Lord, 'plans to prosper you and not to harm you, plans to give you hope and a future.'* The verses that follow are hardly ever quoted at the same time: *'Then, you will call upon me and come and pray to me, and I will listen to you. You will seek me and find me when you seek me with all your heart.'* Even with the addition of those two verses, I am aware that I am taking words out of their context. Nevertheless, this is God speaking, in the days of the Old Covenant, so I cannot believe that he offers anything less valuable than those words to people who faithfully follow him in the present time of New Covenant.

What he promises is the assurance that he has our lives clearly in focus, that through the pains and traumas he will prove himself willing and capable of producing good outcomes, and that for a true disciple of Jesus there is always hope, and there is always a bright future. My responsibility is to be wholehearted in seeking his presence, being open and honest with him, and following his lead into the future which he ultimately controls.

Recovery from bereavement is not reverting to exactly how things were. It is, rather, peeling away all the negatives that MND forced on to my life, and finding fresh ways to embrace life. I have yet to fulfil my potential as a human being and as a follower of Jesus. I have been able to take up again activities that I have enjoyed in the past, such as choral singing. But I now have the freedom to pursue new interests (without feeling that I should consult Gwen first!). I have no doubt that she would encourage me to do what I did in October/November of 2021, which was to be part of a church home group, learning how to bake. I had never previously baked in my life, but when it was included in a variety of different activities on offer for a two-month session of life groups, I signed up. Creativity has never been my strongest suit, but this kind of creative task definitely appealed, especially as the tutor was a lady with infinite patience and a sense of fun. And we could eat the end product!

I know that some people were surprised at how soon I participated again in church activities. In fact, everyone's lives had been clamped to some degree by the coronavirus pandemic, with a nation in lockdown. Church in-person gatherings were banned and we did not meet together as a fellowship until the last Sunday in March 2021, almost four months after Gwen's passing. And the speaker on that Restart Sunday was…. me! We had used recorded talks for many weeks from both our own array of preachers and from those living at a distance. It was easy enough to have a speaker make a video recording of themselves speaking, then send it on to us to go out on the church's website and on YouTube. One benefit was that it reduced travelling expenses to nil for those who would otherwise have come to us from Leicester, Cardiff or even Norway. Another benefit was that church members who rarely left their homes because of age or disability were able to be as much involved as anybody else. And we could send out our services and sermons beyond the regular church membership.

28. How to mourn?

SO HOW SOON after a bereavement should we engage again in normal routines of life?

When I was seventeen, my eldest brother John died from cancer at the age of twenty-six. I was then in the Sixth Form at school and was a regular in the rugby First XV. A match was scheduled against Southport Rugby Club the day after John died, and my parents kindly said it was up to me whether I played or not. I quickly decided it would not be right to play, so I rang the team captain to let him know and to wish the team all the best.

In those days, at the end of the 1950s, a death brought many things to a standstill. Curtains would be drawn in the front room windows of the deceased person's house. Men wore black ties, women had black dresses. Some would deny themselves their favourite radio or television programmes, opting for sombre music rather than anything light-hearted. When a funeral cortege passed along the street, pedestrians would stand at the kerbside with hats removed and heads bowed. These and other traditions were seen as a 'mark of respect' for the dead person. The family would decide how long the period of mourning should last, but nobody was keen to rush back to normality without being seen to observe these rituals for several days, at least.

Changed attitudes today would now regard it as acceptable for a professional sportsman to take part in a fixture within a day or two of a relative's passing. Many people these days are bareheaded, so I cannot remember when I last saw someone remove headgear as a hearse passed by. At many funeral services nowadays those attending are specifically requested not to wear black. That may be because the deceased person was a Christian and the family want to emphasise their quiet joy that the loved one has passed through to the glorious presence of the Saviour they have worshipped. But even for non-believers, there may be a wish to 'give them a happy send-off' to whatever they hope will be the reality beyond the grave.

Shortly before I completed the second draft of this book, Her Majesty Queen Elizabeth II passed away at the age of 96. It cannot be a total surprise when someone of such advanced years dies, but only two days before, she had been accepting the resignation of one Prime Minister of the United Kingdom and then inviting another – the fifteenth of her reign – to form a new government.

What struck me about the series of events that unfolded was how well prepared the leaders in our national life must have been for such an eventuality. Protocols began to unroll like clockwork. In the House of Commons, the new

Prime Minister and the Leader of the Opposition were beginning to debate an extremely serious measure that the Government wanted to implement to help individuals and businesses to cope with huge rises in the costs of fuel. Messages were passed along front rows of Members of Parliament, causing the Leader of the Opposition to slip out and return a few minutes later wearing a black tie. At that stage, the news media were reporting that the Queen's health was giving her doctors concern, but it was a few more hours before we heard that Her Majesty had passed away.

All the main television channels had immediately slashed their normal schedules and presented rolling 'News Specials', in which action was very scarce and talking heads proliferated. Two European club football matches did go ahead, presumably because fans had already arrived from abroad: a minute's silence was impeccably observed before those games and players wore black armbands. Some sports events were immediately cancelled, both on the day the Queen died and in days following, although the people in charge of each sport had the freedom to choose how to proceed. Television presenters had presumably rehearsed their roles in anticipation of this day, as they seemed to know very quickly what the timetable of events would be, leading up to the day of the state funeral.

One sensed that we were observing history in the making, and it was no surprise that the full machinery of the state in all its forms was in motion. Every television presenter and their guests wore black for the next ten days, until the funeral. There was a remarkable symmetry about the installation of a new Prime Minister being followed just two days later by the accession to the throne of King Charles III. Tradition provided continuity and unity when the nation most needed it.

The British royal family are well versed in how to behave in public, and as a nation we have a reputation for the 'stiff upper lip', so there were no great shows of emotion as the sequence of events took place. The new King and some of his relatives were interviewed to express their appreciation of Her late Majesty, and although the mood was sombre, their recollections also included occasions of laughter. One wonders how emotional they all were in private, either in each other's company or on their own. Some would say there is little cause for grief when a life well lived comes to its end after ninety-six years; nevertheless, she was a mother, a grandmother and a great-grandmother, as well as being held so dear by millions of people in Britain and across the world.

29. Exploring emotions

I READ SOMEWHERE THAT however wide a range of emotions we may seem to have, there are in essence just four, which can be summed up as sad, mad, glad and scared. My own experience of Gwen's illness and death would certainly include all four.

One of the saddest aspects was not just what happened to her, but what couldn't now happen, what experiences she would have enjoyed but which were now denied her. She would miss out on grandchildren performing in school plays or choirs, or taking part in sports teams or dance groups; grandchildren getting married and having children; church events; travels abroad or in this country. Also sad was her gradual withdrawal from communal life, particularly church life, as MND stole her powers of speech.

Sadness is easily evoked in recalling shared experiences that we might have repeated, but I am glad and grateful that we did revisit the Isle of Man and enjoy a few days in the Isles of Scilly, both of which were long-held hopes for Gwen. We had no idea that those wishes would be fulfilled within a couple of years of her departure.

Facebook is responsible for prompting tears of sadness when it reminds me of posts from years ago. I recently cried as I watched a short video clip of Gwen, sitting on the floor in our lounge, tooting a kazoo and trying to get our youngest grandchild to copy her. Iris was probably about 18 months old and she shared her grandma's delight when she finally managed a real toot of her own.

Favourite expressions are also liable to make me cry. I had workmen recently stripping and re-doing some rendering on my garage; not a big job, but as always, they were thorough, not just with the rendering but also with cleaning up afterwards. As the last workman let me know he was leaving, I thanked him and said, 'A good job done.' Which is exactly what Gwen used to say to me when I had just mowed the lawn or cleaned some windows. For a couple of minutes I just sat and wept at the poignancy of the memory.

The sadness can easily slide into anger. I don't think I ever became mad with God directly, although there were times when I wrestled with the questions about God's plans for our lives. When God said, 'I know the plans I have for you…', some people emphasise the plural word 'plans'. In a world afflicted by sin and disease, and if we all have freedom to choose a particular life-journey, can there be just one plan for my life? Or does God actually have a range of options – and he knows in advance which pathway I will choose – which may need to be modified because of my mistakes and wrong choices?

I think I would get mad at God if I felt that he had forced on me a particular pathway through life. Discerning the balance between his sovereignty and my freedom of choice can be problematic, but I choose to believe that in his Fatherly goodness he weaves even my mistakes and bad choices into the plan he has for my life.

A hymn I sang often in my younger days in the Methodist Church has a sentimentality that is typical of some of the hymn-writers of the nineteenth century, but I believe the underlying message is correct:-

> In heavenly love abiding,
> No change my heart shall fear,
> And safe is such confiding,
> For nothing changes here:
> The storm may roar without me,
> My heart may low be laid,
> But God is round about me,
> And can I be dismayed?
>
> Wherever He may guide me,
> No want shall turn me back;
> My Shepherd is beside me,
> And nothing can I lack:
> His wisdom ever waketh,

His sight is never dim;
He knows the way He taketh,
And I will walk with Him.

Green pastures are before me,
Which yet I have not seen;
Bright skies will soon be o'er me,
Where the dark clouds have been.
My hope I cannot measure,
My path to life is free;
My Saviour has my treasure,
And he will walk with me.

[Anna Laetitia Waring, 1820-1910]

Some say you can't be certain of things invisible, but for me the adventure of the Christian life is to walk into each new day with a deep assurance of God's presence in my life. In the time since Gwen's promotion to glory I have found a greater sensitivity to the promptings of God's Spirit. Sometimes it's a nudge towards something or somebody I might not have had in mind at a particular moment. Sometimes it's as if a door I was about to go through swings – quite gently – back into my face, causing me to check for a moment the course of action I was about to take. More often than not, I then find another possibility coming to mind, which has the stamp of the Spirit on it and I am able to change course without being upset or angry with either God or myself.

Of those four fundamental emotions, I suppose 'scared' is the one many would expect to be uppermost in reflecting on Gwen's passing. I can honestly say that that is not the case: fear simply did not come into the experience of death. I feel sorry for those who don't have any kind of deep assurance about the destination of their loved one, but my mixture of emotions as Gwen breathed her last breaths did not include fear. We tend to fear the unknown, and what the Bible says about death and the hereafter were, I suppose, so much a part of my being that I had a deep assurance of knowing where Gwen now was.

The times I really was scared were the two occasions in the previous month or so when she had been choking, unable to breathe in or out, and I felt helpless. Rubbing between her shoulder blades had no effect and I was reluctant to smack her back because she was so thin and I was afraid of doing damage to her fragile bone structure. She indicated for me to do exactly that, so it was a mixture of praying and smacking that eventually brought some relief. On both occasions I had rung for emergency help and on both occasions the paramedics said I had done the right thing. But yes, I was scared.

In the hospice, however, on her last day among us, I had no fears at all. She was in the best possible environment – the one she had wanted to be her 'departure lounge' – with caring nurses and doctors at hand. I had commented to the doctor that her pulse seemed strong and it was her lungs that were gradually saying, Enough is enough. The moment of departure was peaceful. I cry now as I write these words and recall very vividly the slight double twitch of her jaw as she took her last breath. I had anticipated that I would cry in that situation, but I remained dry-eyed and clear-headed. I was able to summon the nurse and in the next fifteen minutes to make half a dozen phone calls without once being overwhelmed by emotion.

Sad, mad, scared … and glad.

I have already written the list of 'good things' I believe God asked me to write in the days after Gwen's departure. I do not believe that was an exercise in clutching at straws. I suppose I have generally seen life through a positive lens. When a man in the supermarket car park recently commented on 'another awful day' as it was raining, I almost automatically replied, 'Well, at least it's not foggy.' To me, rain may be inconvenient and uncomfortable, but it isn't normally dangerous in the way that fog or ice or high winds are dangerous. I'm grateful to live in a country that has a temperate climate.

I remember a preacher years ago explaining the difference between happiness and joy. He said that happiness depends on your happenings happening to happen in the way you want your happenings to happen! I think he had a point. The pursuit of happiness seems to me a futile exercise, because happiness is a side effect of honest endeavour or providential circumstances.

Joy is different. Joy comes from a deep sense of security, which arises from a conscious relationship with God. I say 'conscious' because I think many people have a vague sense of God being somewhere in or near their lives, but they never take the steps necessary to bring that relationship to the centre of their lives and so they miss the delicious awareness of God's involvement in their day-to-day reality.

Joy – or gladness – is also bound up with gratitude. It's about appreciating all that is good in life and expressing thanks to people or to God for the good things that they do. I really enjoy being able to commend someone for their honesty or their effort or their graciousness under pressure. And to speak or sing praise to God for who he is and what he has done is just so precious. Praising God in tough times is a genuine sacrifice; it doesn't come naturally or easily. But the action of rejoicing will lead to joy. Most people operate in reverse: they feel joy, so they rejoice. A Christian can generate joy by actively rejoicing in God.

The best part is ... that the best part is still to come! God has so many good things in store, some of them to be experienced in this life, with so many more in the life beyond.

The blessing of the Lord makes a person rich, and he adds no sorrow with it. [Proverbs 10: 22 NLT]

If three of the four fundamental emotions have negative connotations – mad, bad, scared – then it is even more important to make as much as possible of gladness. That does not minimise the reality of the other three, but it does indicate a generally positive mind-set.

I was glad when they said to me, Let us go to the house of the Lord [Psalm 122:1]

Weeping may remain for a night, but rejoicing comes in the morning. [Psalm 30:5]

This is the day the Lord has made; let us rejoice and be glad in it. [Psalm 118:24]

30. What of the future?

WOULD I EXPECT to remarry in later life?

Frankly, no. Not long after Gwen's departure I let my church elders know that I would not be looking for a new partner, so that if they ever heard rumours to that effect they would be able to give a definitive answer. I recall a respected Christian speaker years ago who sadly lost his wife to cancer, and some months later he got up to speak to a large Bible Week gathering. He was smiling as he said he understood there were certain well-meaning people who were trying to line up possible ladies to whom he might be attracted, but he had no intention of remarrying.

My words to my church elders were 'How can you replace the irreplaceable?' At one point I was curious to see how many widows and widowers we had on our church's membership list. I went through the list and discovered up to fifteen widowed ladies. I was the only widower. Each of these ladies had admirable qualities, but none of them stirred even the slightest spark of desire in me to spend my remaining years with them. And too much adapting would be needed in any lady from outside the church who might be attractive to me. I was approaching 80, not 18, so that the compromises necessary to make a success of a new relationship would probably be beyond me.

Not that I didn't occasionally crave female company. Many churches have a preponderance of females over males, and ours was no different in that regard. In the worship team we have always had mainly male instrumentalists and mainly female vocalists, so I was mixing with some ladies there. Likewise, in the Life Group setting – whether it was baking or abstract art – the leaders were ladies and most group members also.

Gwen said more than once before she died that I should be free to form a new attachment if it happened and she would have no objection. I think she was a bit concerned about my ability to cope on my own with advancing years, but she had given me some basic cooking tips and I was already familiar with the washing machine and the ironing board. She did say that I should have somebody in to clean the house, but at the time of writing I have not yet felt the need to do that. Friday morning always was, and continues to be, the time when I do the dusting and hoovering and clean the bathroom. And I am often on the alert to spot cobwebs! I even remember – sometimes – to water the various pot plants that we have had in the house for several years.

I hear of people 'downsizing', as my brother Paul and his wife Pat did some years ago. I suppose a bungalow such as theirs would have its advantages, but the experts tell us that going up and down stairs is good for the heart. Should I think of moving before I have to? A very good question. At the time of writing I feel I can stay on top of housework and basic gardening. I have learnt to enjoy preparing my meals and even doing an occasional bake. I still ride my bike quite regularly as my principal form of exercise. I think I can claim to be as mentally sharp as I was thirty years ago.

'But I trust in you, O Lord; I say "You are my God." My times are in your hands. [Psalm 31: 14-15]

31. Final reflections

THE PERFECT WORLD which God created for the human race to enjoy was spoilt by man's desire for independence. Disease and death, resulting from what the Bible calls sin, have consequently afflicted every generation from then until now. It is not just the tectonic plates which have fault lines close to the surface of the planet; the moral and spiritual fault lines are just as real in the interaction between individuals and nations. There is nothing arbitrary about the words of Jesus that 'in this world you will have trouble'; to be born on the earth is to face the risk of danger, disease and death at any moment. However, Jesus added this reassurance to that statement: 'But take heart! I have overcome the world.' [John 16: 33] How we adjust to that reality makes all the difference between a life of doom and gloom and a life of faith and adventure.

Some questions cannot be fully answered while 'we see things imperfectly as in a poor mirror, but then we will see everything with perfect clarity. All that I know now is partial and incomplete, but then I will know everything completely, just as God knows me now.' [1 Corinthians 13:12 New Living Translation] My question is: Do I need to know everything now? Or can I happily take some things on trust until everything is revealed?

I don't know why or how Gwen contracted motor neurone disease. I read in Acts 12 what happened to two of the closest followers of Jesus, and I have no idea why James was killed by the sword on the orders of King Herod, whereas Peter – next in line for Herod's brutality – had an angelic visitor who released him from chains and quietly escorted him out through locked prison doors and gates. Why was one apostle martyred and the other miraculously spared for further ministry? I don't know, but I don't really need to know.

There are many things in this life that I do not understand: electricity is one, yet I am quite content to have my life eased by a cooker, a washing machine, an iron and a kettle that run on electricity. I cannot claim a full understanding of the internal combustion engine, but I have happily driven tens of thousands of miles in a car. I suppose it is the case that if we understand something, we feel we have a measure of control; but do we really need to understand everything?

I have climbed a fair number of mountains over the years and never lost the sense of exhilaration that comes from placing one's feet on a summit. Life has also given me plenty of emotional and spiritual highs, which are good to remember and for which I am eternally grateful. But we are all going to have to face the lows of the valleys as well. Bunyan's Pilgrim travelled via the Slough of Despond. But he didn't stay there. He kept on going, and so must we. The valley is usually the more fruitful place for vegetation to grow; the peaks of the mountains I have climbed have been mostly barren rock with maybe a thin covering of grass.

If God leads me into a valley, I have to believe there is both purpose in it and a way through.

> *Even though I walk through the valley of the shadow of death, I will fear no evil, for you are with me; your rod and your staff, they comfort me.* [Psalm 23: 4]

In a very real sense Gwen and I walked through the valley of the shadow of death for two years and four months, at the end of which the shadow became reality for Gwen. Yet it was our deep conviction – and for me, it still is – that we both would come through the valley. She has now entered a greater reality which is far more wonderful than our earthbound imaginations can picture. Our guarantee of that reality is the historical fact that two thousand years ago a man called Jesus, who was certified as dead, became alive again three days later. He was recognised by many people, ate and talked with some of them, and allowed them to touch him to be sure they were not hallucinating. Before he was taken up from their sight, he promised that another Person of the Godhead, the Holy Spirit, would soon come to live his life supernaturally in any persons who would make Jesus Christ the central focus of their lives.

It is my sincere hope that anyone reading this book will discover for themselves the peace and joy that come from faith in Jesus, and that his Spirit will lead them in the daily adventure of life as a Christian. And part of that adventure is the assurance that when we find ourselves in a valley, we will surely come through it.